A Boyhood
Nazi Occu

The author as a boy.

A Boyhood Under Nazi Occupation

The Personal Story of Jan Duijvestein

Jan Duijvestein

Foreword by his daughter Janine Barchas,
translator of the Dutch original

EER

Edward Everett Root, Publishers, Brighton, 2020.

EER

Edward Everett Root, Publishers, Co. Ltd.,
30 New Road, Brighton, Sussex, BN1 1BN, England.
edwardeverettroot@yahoo.co.uk
Details of our overseas distributors and how to buy our books
can be seen on our website:
www.eerpublishing.com

A Boyhood Under Nazi Occupation.
The Personal Story of Jan Duijvestein.
Jan Duijvestein

First published in English in Great Britain in 2020.
Translated by Janine Barchas from the author's original Dutch script.
© Jan Duijvestein and Janine Barchas 2020.
This edition © Edward Everett Root Publishers 2020.

ISBN: 978-1-913087-48-7 Paperback
ISBN: 978-1-913087-11-1 Hardback
ISBN: 978-1-913087-12-8 eBook

Cover and Production by Pageset Limited, High Wycombe, Buckinghamshire.

For Madison, my granddaughter

I.H.V.J.
Opa

With this series of anecdotes about the Second World War, stories I told often to my own children, I intend to please those with an interest in this important period of history. In sharing these memories more widely, I allow others to take part in my gift to Madison, my granddaughter in America. When she was born in 1998, I promised her parents to make for her this book. That promise is hereby fulfilled.

Jan Duijvestein
Den Haag
2010

Contents

List of illustrations

Foreword

My father, Jan Duijvestein, was born on 20 October 1931, making him eight years old in May 1940 when the German army, marching under orders of Adolf Hitler, reached the Dutch coast. Seated on a low wall along a main thoroughfare in The Hague, my young father watched with childish curiosity and disbelief as singing German soldiers in high black boots marched into his home town. Thus began the start of the Nazi occupation of Holland, and indeed most of Europe, that would last for five interminable years, until the Germans surrendered in May of 1945.

He spent those five years, age eight to thirteen, growing up under the thumb of Nazi rule. The war coincided with his formative years and being a witness to injustice and deprivation changed him forever. My father, born Johannes Andreas but familiarly dubbed 'Jan' for short, was the fourth child of seven in a large middle-class Catholic family in The Hague, all of whom managed to survive the war—even the aptly-named Hunger Winter of 1944. Son of a substantial wholesaler in fruits and vegetables, my father was roughly Anne Frank's age during the war. Although his experiences bear little or no resemblance to the true horrors and persecution suffered by the Frank family, his recollections convey the dominant sense of deprivation and dread inflicted by Hitler's ruthless occupation upon the Dutch populace.

During my own Dutch childhood, my father told my brother, my sister, and myself stories about the war that he later wrote down to make this book. As children, we savoured these tales about family members whom we knew in a different context. Each of us often asked him to rehearse again their own favourites. Mine was the story of the hidden bicycles and the German *fietsenrazzia* that had frightened my grandmother, whom we called *Moe* and who otherwise seemed so solid and unflappable. Or maybe it was the one about my 12-year-old father setting off on foot to trade a single cigar for a liter of milk at a distant farm. My father was a remarkable raconteur, and I recall being spellbound at every telling and retelling.

My father intended his war stories as important warnings, as grave history lessons in the need for self-reliance, sacrifice, and generosity.

For me, they were my own personal version of Harry Potter before there was a Harry Potter. In these little plots about a world threatened by true evil, a young boy takes over from incapacitated adults who dare not show themselves. My young father, with an intelligence disguised by a cherubic head of blond curls, was often sent out on errands that might, along streets patrolled by German soldiers, have been dangerous for his older teenage sisters or even for his parents. With evil all around, he slips past Nazi guards in the search for what his family needed (nearly always food). Here was a boy with special powers. And this was my own dad! I had constant and incontrovertible proof from my own father that children do not have to wait to be adults to be important. These stories made me hopeful that I, too, might be that important to my own family in a crisis. I kept my pocketknife and allowance inside a handkerchief in a dresser drawer, just in case.

Decades later, when my daughter Madison was born in 1998 in New Zealand, her proud Dutch grandfather said that he wanted to give his first grandchild a useful present and asked for suggestions. My in-laws had just given us a brand-new video camera to lessen geographical distance, and I think he expected me to ask for something practical like a good stroller or fancy crib. Instead, we asked him to write down all the familiar war stories for his granddaughter. At first, he was a reluctant author. It took him a few years to emotionally gear up and then many more of writing by hand in a notebook every day at lunchtime in the lunchroom of a downtown department store. When he was done he hired a typist, located old family photos, and gave the bound, illustrated typescript to Madison in 2010, when she turned 12. Because she was born in New Zealand and is growing up in the United States, I translated his collection for her from Dutch into English.

Encountering these same stories again as an adult, I see that while the plots are exactly the same—almost verbatim what I remember being told when I was little—they read differently now. As an adult I recognize how the Dutch actors in these recollections, including my father, are actually not heroes who make great sacrifices for justice. These are ordinary people trying to feed themselves and their families. These stories record life lived under the cruelties of occupation, when small acts of kindness or defiance sustained the human spirit.

True suffering in his stories occurs off-page. Yet there is something about a slowly accumulating ordinariness in the context of the larger horrors of World War II that makes these stories so consistently powerful. No one at the center behaves with great bravery—and very little actually happens. Life remains bounded by familiar things, ordinary and domestic. But this seemingly ordinary life hovers over some horrid meat grinder that remains just out of sight. Given that wartime context, the power of these stories lies in their extraordinary ordinariness.

Miraculously, in these stories my father comes into brief contact with all of the war's archetypical characters, both good and evil. By chance, his after-school job as an apprentice baker places him beside a prominent member of the Dutch Resistance while a random schoolyard spat brings him into the headmaster's office to face the boy's Nazi father, the Dutch leader of Germany's largest counter intelligence programme. As the headmaster questions him in front of this powerful German sympathizer, my Catholic father just happens to have a Star of David patch in his pocket, plucked that morning on the way to school out of a hedge, where it had been discarded. That moment still gives me chills. Each nail-biting recollection introduces features of the Nazi occupation with a disarming matter-of-factness: ration coupons, bombardments, going into hiding, the constant need to locate sources of food, the lack of electric light, curfews, coats sewn from blankets, secret radio programs, and dangers great and small. These first-hand recollections make the details of living with war palpably real for someone, like me, who has only ever experienced peacetime.

My father died on 14 March 2019, at the age of 87—a few weeks after learning that a publisher in England wanted to make a "real book" out of his wartime stories. When entering the hospice in Voorburg, he extended his hand in greeting to the nursing staff and proudly introduced himself as "Jan Duijvestein, realtor and author." My father had indeed spent his adult life in real estate, both selling and building properties. When the Cold War had threatened his wife and three young children in the 1970s, stirring up childhood memories of a war in Europe, he left Holland and emigrated with his family to the United States. The memories of cheering on the American soldiers who had freed The Hague of the Nazis in May 1945 had seared into his mind a sense of the United States as a place of freedom and safety. Economically, the results of the move to the States proved disastrous. My father had always done his business deals on a handshake and Los Angeles did not prove fully worthy of his trust or loyalty. But his kids thrived in America, even after he eventually returned to Holland in semi-retirement, where for a few more years he ran a souvenir shop in the lobby of a large hotel.

These powerful stories about a boyhood during the German occupation of Holland in World War II are my father's personal stories and memories. Yet, as I and my siblings grew up, they became our stories too—and later those of his grandchildren. These little plots were our first unvarnished history lessons in both human cruelty and dignity. Just as these experiences shaped my father, whose kindness towards others was a recurring motif at his memorial service, the hearing and reading of these stories also shaped his audience. These stories are a worthy legacy. May they teach next generations to remember that great things begin with small deeds.

It has been a special privilege to translate these stories and see them through the publication process with the help of family members who located photos and researched facts. On purpose, I have retained a sprinkling of his Dutch words, names, and expressions (in italics and explained in the glossary at the back), for I do not want the reader of the English text to lose sight of where these stories took place.

I am Jan's eldest daughter and my first name, Janine, is a diminutive of his. I remain "little Jan."

—Janine Barchas
  May 2019
  Austin, Texas

Pictures of our family at the start of the Second World War

Figure 1: My father, Adrianus Daniël Josephus Duijvestein (born 28 December 1903).

Figure 2: My mother, Wilhelmina Johanna Hendriks (born 18 December 1903).

Figure 3: My parents relaxing at our home before the war.

Figure 4: Formal photo of us kids. Gerard (8 April 1934); Klasien (18 Aug 1928); Kees (2 Sept 1930); Jos (8 Aug 1935); Truus (26 Nov 1926); Jan (20 Oct 1931); Adri (13 April 1933). As adults long after the war, four of us Anglicised the spelling of our old-fashioned Dutch names, becoming *Truce*, *Clasine*, *Cees*, and *Josh*.

Figure 5: Informal photo of all seven of us on a wall just before the war. In ascending order of age from L to R: Jos, Gerard, Adri, Jan, Kees, Klasien, and Truus.

Chapter 1
Poverty and unemployment in the 1930s

Before the war even began, many people already had a number of hard years behind them. Unemployment was high and with social services strained beyond capacity much of the population suffered under genuine poverty. These circumstances provide a context for the following anecdote.

My father was a devout Catholic who regularly attended church even on weekdays. One day, as he was leaving early morning services, where he had asked God for better times, he fell into conversation with a total stranger.

'These sure are bad times,' began the man, 'I've been out of work for a few months now.' He followed up with: 'Would you, by any chance, know of any available work for me?'

'Well, what type of work did you do?' asked my father.

'I'm a banker,' answered the man in a rather lofty tone.

My father assumed that the man probably meant that he had simply worked in a bank.

'Yes, these are hard times, but sadly, I cannot help you,' answered my father while he walked in the direction where he had parked his car.

'Would you look at that,' said the man pointing to my father's car. 'The guy who drives that car knows nothing about hardship.'

Without so much as a flicker of recognition, my father walked right past his car as he continued to talk with the man about the bad economy. When they reached the Kwartellaan, the man turned right towards the Laan van Poot while my father continued on to the Vliegervangerlaan, where we lived at number fourteen.

Figure 6: Our original house, which bore the name Wilhelmina, just like my mother who was known to her friends as 'Mien'—at no. 14 Vliegervangerlaan in the coastal Vogelwijk area of Den Haag. This photo was taken by a professional photographer a few days after the forced move took place on 8 December 1942, to serve as a keepsake in case it was demolished. In anticipation, my mother left the front curtains up a few extra days.

After eating breakfast, drinking a second cup of coffee, and reading the paper, he walked back to the church to pick up his car.

My father told me this anecdote from the Depression on several occasions. The story not only resonates with the trouble of those years, but also conveys something of my father's sensitivity.

Chapter 2
The start of the war

When the war began, we lived in the quiet coastal neighbourhood of the Vogelwijk in Den Haag. It started in the early morning of 10 May 1940.

Figure 7: German paratroopers on 10 May 1940, just outside Den Haag.

I remember quite clearly how, at about five in the morning, my parents slid open the curtains of my bedroom, which I shared with my brother Kees. The noise woke me. I recall hearing them whisper as they peered long and hard at the sky. While I was not completely alert or awake yet, my mother noticed that I was no longer fast asleep. When she and my father left the room, she reassured me: 'Don't worry, Jan, you don't have to get up quite yet. You just stay warm and cozy in your bed. I'll come and get you in a couple of hours.'

This bizarre and mundane moment has stayed with me. Only much later did I realise that it marked the start of "The Second World War." This, then, was the moment the Germans invaded our nation.

At the age of eight, I did not of course understand what the consequences of this would be for our country. Soon enough, however, I did realise that unusual things were about to happen.

The radio was on all day, with my parents attentively listening nearby and frequently shushing us to be quiet. Sirens sounded regularly, which was the signal for us all to shelter under the stairs that led up to the second floor. All nine of us would crouch there, pressed closely against one another, waiting for the siren to change to a monotone that signaled that the danger had passed. The space under the stairs, or so I was told, was the safest place to be during a bombardment. Even at eight, I could grasp that.

What I did not fully understand was the scary talk about the enemy's possible use of gas to force us to surrender. But, I was reassured, that would not happen because of agreements made at the 'Geneva Convention.' Still, there were people who were so scared that they filled the gaps and crevices around their doors and windows with rags and old newspapers. At school, our teacher told us that no one was allowed to shoot at parachutists until they had safely reached the ground. I remember thinking that this did not make sense and decided not to believe it.

At the start of the war, people tried in all sorts of ways to limit or avoid the expected damages and destruction of warfare. I remember, for example, being taken aback by flower motifs on many windows. Many people in our neighbourhood taped their windows to try to control the dangerous shards that might otherwise fly around during a bomb explosion. While I thought the use of tape smart, I found it silly that so many people placed it to form fussy flower patterns, rather than just stick it on strong and straight. I even entertained the wicked hope that, in case a bomb should fall in our neighbourhood, it might strike a house where the occupants had been particularly artistic in their application of tape.

Of those first few days, I also recall one evening when I missed my father and asked where he was. I was told that he and a number of our neighbours were helping to erect barricades. He'd been told to bring as much old furniture and stuff from home as possible. I was only eight, but even then I understood that as a country we did not appear to be well-prepared against an attack from the Germans.

My doubt was confirmed when, after only five days, the fight was given up. A voice on the radio, which my father recognized as belonging to the regular news reporter, announced that Holland was forced to surrender. 'This is no false report!' reacted my father, because he recognized the radio announcer's voice.

A few days later, when things had calmed down somewhat, our neighbour, a man with family in Belgium, told us in tears that Belgium, too, had surrendered. I did not understand why the man was crying, because the relative quiet of those last few days had made me think that the war was already over.

My Oma, my father's mother, returned to her own home in the Gallileïstraat, having stayed with us for a week. She hoped to sleep better at home. In our house she'd not been able to sleep because it had proved too quiet! She had missed her own neighbourhood's traffic noises, especially the sound of the tram!

Curious to see the Germans enter the city of Den Haag, I walked to the Sportlaan. Perched atop a low brick wall, I watched the soldiers march past, genuinely fascinated by the spectacle. In full voice, they sang as they marched, sometimes even in two- or three-part harmony: 'Und wir fahren, und wir fahren gegen England, England.' What made their song particularly impressive to me as a boy was the accompanying beat of hundreds of boots hitting the pavement in unison. I do recall wondering why this extraordinary spectacle drew remarkably little public interest, from neither children nor adults.

That evening at the dinner table, it became clear to me why there had been so few people outside watching. 'What an awful sight I encountered this morning,' began my father. He then told us how disgusted and offended he had been by a glimpse of those 'screaming' German soldiers on his morning route to work. His account made me realise that I would do better to keep quiet about what I had been an entranced witness to, sitting on that wall, that morning. The harmonies sung by those many voices, accompanied by the heavy pounding of hundreds of boots, had made an extraordinary impression on me. It was hard to keep silent about it.

Those five days following the 10th of May 1940 had, of course, been strange days for us kids. Oma Duijvestein, our paternal grandmother had stayed with us while sirens had blared constantly. Not to be allowed to play outside was, in and of itself, most unusual.

Figure 8: I remember well the tight formation, heavy boots, and song of the German soldiers. In this photo, taken in Den Haag that same day in May 1940, notice how very few people grant them an audience. Beeldbank WO2 – NIOD (161791)

How odd that, after 70 years, it is so easy to recall the events of those first few days. I can see us, huddled once again under the stairs in response to a siren's blare, as the kitchen door flew open. It was merely the green grocer, making his weekly rounds to see if my mother needed anything. What a relief when he called out 'It's the grocer!'

We'd been told that some German soldiers, dressed as ordinary Dutch citizens, were parachuting out of their airplanes in order to mingle with the Dutch people and promote chaos and confusion from within. If you did not trust someone's identity, the story went, you should ask them to repeat the following expression: '*Scheveningse scheepsbeschuit*'. For a German this Dutch tongue-twister was an impossible utterance. Whether this phrase served as a true litmus test of citizenship, I do not know, but it was one of many such stories making the rounds in those early days.

In any case, I was mightily glad that the man who fell, as it were, in our midst while we huddled under the stairs was merely 'our' grocer and not some disguised German.

Chapter 3
The move to Voorburg

When I think back on the initial years of the war, I have to admit that, with the exception of those first five anxious and chaotic days, things were fairly uneventful for us. What was unnerving was how the occupiers employed various tactics to keep the public calm and in check. Rather than announce bad news directly, the Germans deliberately leaked and manipulated news events that might prove unpleasant for the populace.

For example, in 1942 there was a rumour that our coastal neighbourhood, the Vogelwijk, was to be emptied. Only ten years old, our neighbourhood was a relatively new development that lay directly behind the dunes. It was to be completely flattened, or so the rumour went. In the event of an invasion from allied troops, the Germans would then be better able to fend off an attack. This plan was but a small part of a long coastline of defenses called the 'Atlantic wall', concerning a distance of some 2685 kilometers—from Norway via Denmark, Holland, and Belgium, down to the French-Spanish border.

People reacted with dismay, exclaiming:

'To destroy a whole neighbourhood, with homes only ten years old?'
'This surely cannot be true'.
'Where are we supposed to go?'
'No, that won't happen!'

We were therefore glad, and not all too surprised, when that initial rumour was soon contradicted and denied by the occupying forces themselves. No, of course there were no plans to empty out the Vogelwijk. Everyone believed them, and calm returned to the neighbourhood.

All this was, my father told us, a tactical strategy deployed by the Germans. By deliberately spreading and then countermanding a rumour about a possible destruction of the neighbourhood, they hoped to give everyone a chance to adjust to the possibility—making things easier for the occupiers when time came to move people out.

With posters stuck to trees and buildings, the details of an official

German 'Befehl,' or command, was eventually announced. These posters also listed the sanctions deployed against anyone would did not obey the order to leave.

It proved that my father, upon first hearing of these rumours, had immediately gone in search of another home suitable for a family with seven children. He had found one in Voorburg, on the Laan van Nieuw Oosteinde at 269, and had bought the house. We moved in several months later.

Figure 9: Our new house at no. 269 along the Laan van Nieuw Oosteinde in the Voorburg neighbourhood.

After these preparations, it was therefore no great shock to my own father when, a few months after the initial rumour had been so vehemently denied, he received an official order to vacate our house. We were given only two weeks to leave the house in the Vogelwijk. Within as many months the whole neighbourhood was emptied. Many families moved in with others. In some cases, households were split up, with some children placed with relatives here and others there.

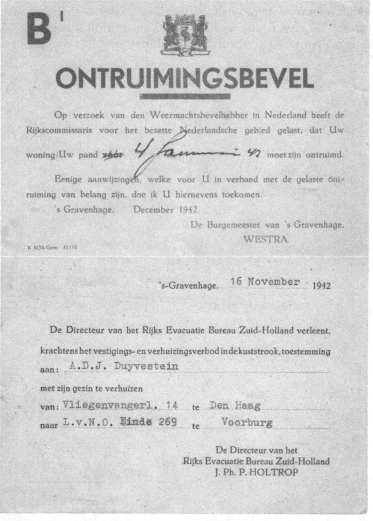

Figure 10: Official eviction notice to move out of our home in the Vogelwijk district in December 1942 and the separate permit to move to another address.

When my father told the back neighbours that we would be moving in a couple of days, the man reacted sharply: 'Yah, well you have it easy. You have another home to go to. I have to move my family into an empty school building.'

My father was polite enough not to remind the man of what he had said a few months earlier in reaction to being told that we'd bought another house. At that time, he had chided: 'What? You've bought another house, just because of that rumour? Haven't you heard that the Germans are now saying it isn't true? You sure are easily scared.' Why would my father want to rub that in? Things were bad enough already.

Chapter 4
Farewell to my old neighbourhood

It seemed as if lessons at school lasted longer than usual. That was probably because I was constantly thinking about the upcoming move. It was an exciting prospect to have to bike, together with my brothers, to the other side of town—all the way to Voorburg! Another house. A different school where I would make new friends. It all seemed so thrilling.

In addition, I took with me the happy memories of a carefree youth in the Vogelwijk. For me and many other children, life had continued on with seeming normalcy, in spite of the fact that we were now an occupied country.

In the lower school, where I had spent five years, Paul Vollebregt and Appie Ruysgrok were my best friends.

Certain classmates you never forget. Like that boy, whose name I do not recall, but who made such an impression upon me by daring, when he had been justly punished and made to stand in the corner, to turn around and yell rudely at the teacher: 'I'm going to tell my father, and then you'll be sorry!' He was a boy whose father was a member of the hated N.S.B. party, a group sympathizing with the Germans. We never heard anything more about any consequences from this incident.

But I did understand, from the stories told at home, that it was better, even when you were young, to be careful about what you told other people. Although my own daily life remained relatively untainted by the war during its initial phase, terrible things were happening all around us—about which my father told me in later years.

As a boy of eleven, for example, I had not yet heard of 'executions.' I certainly could not imagine then what an event like that would mean for a family confronted with it.

One day, we did hear that the neighbour who had lived across the street from us in the Vliegenvangerlaan, and who was known to us kids as

'Bally', had been 'picked up'. We called him Bally because he traded in shoes, especially the famous Swiss brand. His last name was actually Smit.

Figure 11: Propaganda poster for the N.S.B. in 1940. 'No division by parties, but a united people.'

Meneer Smit was picked up because of his work for the resistance movement. He falsified papers, helping certain people to stay out of the hands of the Germans. First, he was taken to the well-known prison in Scheveningen, which in the vernacular became known as *Het Oranjehotel,* or 'Orange Hotel', for holding so many members of the resistance (those loyal to the Dutch crown were associated with the color orange). Eventually, he was executed.

Figure 12: Main entrance of the coastal prison at Scheveningen, dubbed The Orange Hotel during the war.

He therefore never knew that, meanwhile, he'd become the father of a longed-for son. It later proved that the underground had collected money and gold in an effort to purchase the freedom of Meneer Smit.

Thirty years after the liberation, in 1975, Meneer Smit was posthumously recognized for his sacrifice. I was told this by my then-neighbour Meneer Van Leeuwen, who worked for the N.I.O.D., the Dutch institute for war documentation. I could not imagine how this award, bestowed so many years later, might be meaningful for his descendants.

I was proved wrong when, by chance in 1980, I met the daughter of Meneer Smit in Los Angeles. The family had been decidedly pleased with the posthumous recognition and had celebrated it with a festive dinner over which their mother had proudly presided.

Chapter 5
Hear, see, and be silent

The move from the Vogelwijk to Voorburg had been completed, and without mishap. We quickly adjusted to our new home and environs, including a new school and parish church.

It was true that in the evenings over dinner my father increasingly cautioned us about how we should behave in front of strangers. He insisted that we be extremely careful about what we confided in others, including how we felt about the Germans.

In turn, my father told us about what he knew or thought of our new neighbours in Voorburg. According to him, on one side we had 'good' neighbours, while on the other side he could not yet tell what kind they were, for he had not yet met them. As a result, I behaved with increased caution and became obsessively observant— even though still a child.

This is why I remember that at the home of my new classmate, Ben Pas, I saw a small frame with a picture of Queen Wilhelmina. Underneath the photo was the following text: 'No, it was not flight that led you away, but the voice of God calling you.' Although I did not much admire the escape of our sovereign (she and her family fled to England in the first days of the war) and so struggled a little with the sense of the text, I did recognize that this picture meant that the Pas family sympathised with the Dutch royals. These were therefore 'good' people.

To confirm our shared 'good'-ness, Ben and I agreed, at my suggestion, to make and wear a special pin. The pin had a little crown at the top, with underneath the letter **J** for Juliana (the crown princess) and a **B** for Bernhard (her husband). If we were ever asked about the meaning of this pin, we could always say that this referred to the **J** for Jan and the **B** for Ben. We did not have any alternative explanation for the little crown.

At Ben's home, there also stood a dresser proudly arranged with a group of framed family photos, among them a picture of our queen with a unique text running along the side:

21

Wij	[We]
Weerloze	[Defenseless]
Wandelaars	[Wanderers]
Wij	[We]
Weten	[Know]
Wat	[What]
Wij	[We]
Willen	[Want]
Wij	[We]
Willen	[Want]
Wilhelmientje	[Wilhelmina]
Weer.	[Back]

Figure 13: Queen Wilhelmina in 1942.

This memory about the Pas family would have taken place in 1943. Whether the picture of our queen remained on the dresser for the remainder of the war, I don't know. The Germans were increasingly aggressive, capable of detaining, or in extreme cases even executing, people who displayed their Orange sympathies too openly on their clothing or even in their own home.

The Pas family owned a grocery store along the Herengracht in Den Haag. With the slogan '*Dat komt van Pas*' their business advertised the usefulness of their wares [this simultaneously translates into 'this comes in useful' as well as 'this comes from the Pas store']. Fond of puns, I thought their slogan tremendously clever.

Ben eventually told me that during the final phase of the war the family sold the right to use their unique business slogan to a colleague in the grocery business. Instead of money, the deal was struck in exchange for groceries.

This sale hints at the increasing deprivations during the last years of the war, when the shortage of food reduced life to mere 'surviving.' Even the sale of a business slogan so integral to the Pas family identity was used to increase their odds of survival.

Chapter 6
Bad sorts

It must have been towards the end of 1943 that I was playing with my by-then best friend Ben Pas on the street in front of his house, as we often did.

At one point, another boy joined our game. Like Ben, he lived in the Amalia van Solmsstraat and was in our grade at school. I knew the boy, although we were not particularly close or even friendly, probably because his father, whose name was Poos, was a member of the hated N.S.B. political party. I had seen the man often enough in his black uniform, with those large shiny black boots.

I don't remember why, but our game turned into a mighty quarrel, in which the son of Poos called me names and screamed: 'Your mother goes with an N.S.B.-er!' I remember how ridiculous and hurtful I found the accusation. My own mother—married to my father—was not someone whom anyone should say nasty things about. Angry, I retaliated, shouting: 'Your sister goes with and N.S.B.-er! And that is the truth, because I saw it for myself.'

Our fight pretty much ended there, and so I had no idea why, a few days later, I was suddenly summoned out of our classroom and asked to report to the office of the head of school, de heer Van Huysduinen. Unaware of having committed any wrongdoing, I obeyed the summons. While walking down the stairs, I noticed that the door to the head of school's office stood wide open.

The first thing I saw as I entered the office was a large pair of shiny black boots. When I took a better look, I also registered the telltale black riding pants and black button-down shirt, crossed by a black shoulder belt. I barely noticed the head of school, since I froze at the sight of the man in this black uniform.

I recognized him immediately: this was unmistakably *Meneer* Poos, the father of the boy with whom I'd quarreled. 'This is Meneer Poos,' began the head of school. 'Meneer Poos would like to know what you and his son are quarreling about.'

I was somewhat relieved by the question and earnestly and quickly explained to them both how the son of Meneer Poos had started the fight by accusing my mother of going with an N.S.B-er, which was a ridiculous accusation. In response, I had said that his sister did go with an N.S.B.-er, and that this *was* true because I had seen it myself.

My relief at the question was partly the result of my own theory about why I might have been called before these men in the office of the head of school. That morning on the way to school I had found a cloth Star of David in the hedge near the tram stop. It was in my pocket. Although I had told no one, I still assumed that this was why I was being questioned. I was relieved, then, when it proved that there was another reason.

I don't remember exactly what the head of school told me in response to my answer, but the sum of it was that we were too young to meddle in that sort of thing and that, above all, I should keep in mind that Meneer Poos was a powerful man. I was told to shake the hand of Meneer Poos and to promise that, henceforth, we would stick to playing games.

Throughout the war, Poos, together with his partner Slagter, worked on the side of the Germans in their fight against the resistance. In this manner they betrayed many members of the underground movement to the Germans, sending them to their deaths. The two of them were also involved in 'Das Englandspiel.' They would pick up secret British agents who parachuted into Holland, pretending to help them. The opposite was true. They extracted from these brave men any and all information, precisely in order to pass it on to the Germans. After the liberation, the two were held accountable for hundreds of such arrests. Most of their victims had not survived the war.

Figure 14: A list of collaborators, or *verraders*, constructed by the Dutch Resistance, shows Poos and Slagter. Beeldbank WO2 – NIOD (76724).

After the war, in 1948, L.A. Poos was sentenced to death for war crimes, although the verdict was reduced to life imprisonment in 1951. In 1962, Poos was, along with his colleague Slagter, released.

Chapter 7
Anti-Semitism

After the first two years of the war, the mood became increasingly grim. By then, it was clear that the occupiers intended to tighten their stranglehold on the populace. By April 1941, the Germans announced that anyone aged sixteen and older always had to carry personal documentation—papers to prove their identity.

In addition to a picture, such a document showed fingerprints, making it harder to falsify. Attempts to alter the information in such a document were easy to spot, because the thin layer of cellophane over one fingerprint betrayed any tampering. That would make the papers immediately invalid.

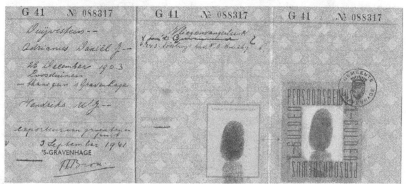

Figure 15: Examples of the personal identification certificates made mandatory from 1941 onwards. These *persoonsbewijzen* belonged to my father and (shown on next page) his mother, G. M. van der Arend.

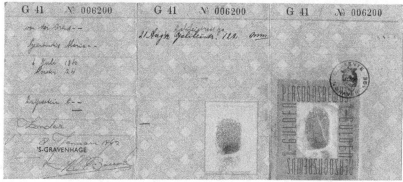

For the Jewish citizens, in January of 1942, came the directive to report in, which resulted in the letter **J** being placed inside their personal identification papers. Shortly thereafter, they were also obliged to display on their clothing a cotton yellow Star of David when in public. The star held the word *Jood*, or Jew.

When, one day on the way to school I found such a star in the hedge at the end of the tramline, the edges of the sewing ragged from where it had been ripped off a coat or shirt, I tucked it deep into the pocket of my pants. I did not show it to anyone. This was the same day that I was called in to report to the head of school about having had an argument with another boy, whose father was the infamous N.S.B.-er, Poos. That night I flushed the Star of David down the toilet.

With increasing frequency there were signs that barred entry to Jews: '*Voor Joden Verboden.*' In addition, it was now widely known that those Jews who, heeding official calls, did report in to the German authorities were being transported to labour camps. It was during this time that

I first heard about 'Auschwitz' in Poland, a country that had been in the possession of the Germans slightly longer. There were all sorts of stories circulating about the atrocities committed there.

Figure 16: Example of a Star of David patch that Jews were forced to wear. Beeldbank WO2 – NIOD (96962).

Figure 17: Example of the signs barring entrance to Jews. Beeldbank WO2 – NIOD (97056).

Around this time, when an illness of my father's prompted a house call from our doctor, I overheard a hallway conversation between my mother and the doctor—after he had finished examining my father. Their whisperings in the downstairs hallway had so raised my curiosity that I sat on the top step of our curved stairs, in order to quietly listen in. That is when I heard of medical experiments in Auschwitz being conducted on prisoners. For example, the bodies of prisoners were being pumped full of water to see how much a human body could hold before it exploded!

Because I had deliberately listened in on a private conversation, I could not begin to ask my mother about what I had heard. Of that I was certain. But on Sundays in church I kept wondering with increasing frequency why there were no sermons about what was happening to the Jews. Why not ask us all to help them, perhaps by sheltering a few in our homes or placing them in hiding? 'Why is there so little resistance to the Germans?' I often wondered. I also asked myself, while sitting in church, why the Pope did not simply excommunicate all German soldiers. Surely that would be a way to make the Catholic Church's position clear.

Meanwhile, the Germans did everything to sour the lives of the Jews. They even circulated derogatory stories to cultivate anti-Semitic feelings among the non-Jewish population. For example, one story that made the rounds concerned a Jew who had to go into hiding with the help of a close acquaintance. He asked his friend to keep a suitcase full of brand new shoes safe for him. The friend felt mistrusted and insulted when, upon opening the suitcase, he discovered that it only contained shoes for the left foot. It was said that, as a result, this man had nothing good to say about the Jew whom he helped. At first, I thought it a rather clever trick. But when I thought about it some more, I agreed that it was a rotten thing to do. It was precisely that final feeling, an antipathy for the Jewish people, which the Germans wished to cultivate in us.

Years later, after our country was again free, I began to study for the profession of realtor. In order to learn the trade, I volunteered as an apprentice at the realty office of Wolf and Luirink, which lay along the Keizersgracht in Amsterdam. My take-home pay amounted to 60 guilders a month. Since my monthly train pass to Amsterdam cost me precisely 61 guilders, I was essentially working for free.

One day, I was allowed to accompany the boss to an official valuation of the property located at Prinsegracht No. 263. As a former leader of the resistance, my boss had been asked to view this property and report on its condition. At that moment, I did not know that the building would eventually become famous as the Anne Frank Huis. It was this building that, starting in 1942, had sheltered Anne Frank and her family, along with a small group of other Jewish persons. These people remained there, in hiding, until they were betrayed in 1944, picked up, and shipped to concentration camps. Only when, some time later, I read the published diary of Anne Frank, did I realise the building's true historical significance.

Figure 18: The now famous house of Anne Frank along the Prinsengracht in Amsterdam. Beeldbank WO2 – NIOD.

Back at the office, I related where I had been with some measure of excitement. That afternoon I had to type up the official report for our client, which advised against any purchase of the property due to the building's poor condition. Overriding this advice, the Anne Frank Foundation nonetheless decided to go forward with a purchase that included the building next door, in order to create the now world-famous museum. I think it a great privilege to have walked around that particular building so soon after the war's end.

Many years after that, I wanted to take my then-business partner from America, Ben Chernick, to the museum. Ben was Jewish and particularly interested in visiting the Anne Frank House. I remember that we arrived around five o'clock to find it already closed. Just as we were asking ourselves 'What now?' we were addressed by a young man from behind the closed museum door, who called out: 'Wir sind geschlossen!'

I would have accepted such an announcement in any foreign language but German! The harsh German shout in this building with this particular history seemed decidedly irreverent.

Chapter 8
Herr Wuppermann

In 1943, the Germans began to requisition automobiles. What seemed an outlandish rumour at the start eventually became reality. Every car owner was expected to blithely turn in his vehicle. My father was the proud owner of what, at that time, was considered a handsome 1936 Dodge coupe.

Figure 19: My father's pride was this 1936 Dodge that he so cleverly managed to hide from the Germans. Here it is parked in front of our house after the war.

He conceived of the idea of hiding his car in one of the two warehouses in Loosduinen that he leased as part of his import and export business in produce. My father traded in wholesale vegetables and fruits. His business was at a standstill because of the war, like nearly all businesses in the agricultural sector. That meant that the large auction halls and warehouses were little trafficked and virtually abandoned, which made them a great place to hide his car. But, of course, no one should see the car enter the auction compound.

My father knew that the compound was watched over by a guard, placed there to prevent theft and fire. He also knew that this man, who happened to be German by birth, made his inspection around the terrain at six o'clock every morning. This is why my father decided to sneak his car into the warehouse as early as five. Driving the car slowly into the darkened compound, he was shocked when he recognized Herr Wuppermann, for that was the guard's name, standing in the beams of his headlights.

My father was smart enough to pause and enthusiastically greet Herr Wuppermann, rather than drive straight through to the warehouse. After a long chat, he drove his Dodge into the back of the warehouse, piling at least fifty empty vegetable crates in front of it. The wooden crates made a tall wall through which the car was no longer visible. Getting on his bicycle (which he had brought with him), my father rode back to the watchman, presenting him with a cigar before calmly peddling away.

From that moment on, only two people knew that there was a car hidden from the occupying Germans in that warehouse. My father was convinced that the watchman would not betray him, partly because the man would understand that he had been the only witness. Should the Germans enter the compound and drive straight to the warehouse to confiscate the hidden car, he would know that Wuppermann had been the one to tell them where to find it. The watchman, who was well-respected generally, never told, which is why even after the war my father remained the proud owner of the same Dodge coupe.

Some years later, my father boasted of how, while filling his tank at a petrol station in 1946, a total stranger had made him an offer on the car that was much higher than the vehicle's original price. That was not all that unusual, since immediately after the war it was almost impossible to find a car for purchase. Even some time later, you could do so only if you had a permit.

When, in 1947, my father was traveling through Germany on business and was stopped along a checkpoint in the road and asked for his papers, the official approvingly remarked 'Du hast ein schönes Auto.' Given the car's history and his wily plan to prevent it from becoming a German possession, the remark registered as humorous.

That same year, we were surprised when my father hired a German to be a new lorry driver in his fleet of delivery trucks, especially because it was know that this man had served in the German army. The young driver was named Frans Wuppermann. His father had pleaded with my father to hire him.

Frans ended up working at my father's company for about 30 years. I can still see him crying on the day of my father's funeral.

Chapter 9

The baker on the corner who never returned

I was twelve when I learned many expressions specific to the war, such as: 'illegality', 'samenschoolingsverbod', 'Het Oranjehotel', 'going into hiding', 'black market', and 'bukshag'. I understood their meanings fairly quickly. That is not to say, however, that as a child I understood why these things happened as they did.

Near our house, on the corner of the Laan van Nieuw Oosteinde and the Bilderdijklaan (which would later be renamed Koningin Julianalaan), was the *banketbakkerij* of Henk van Elewout. To me, of course, he was *Meneer* van Elewout, a bachelor in his late thirties who ran a bakery business in cakes and sweets.

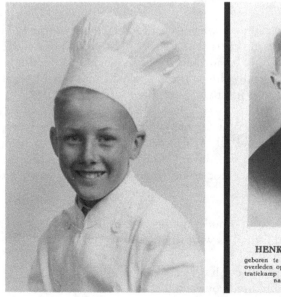 

BID VOOR MIJ
HENK VAN ELEWOUT,
geboren te 's-Gravenhage 15 April 1906,
overleden op 16 April 1945 in het Concen-
tratiekamp Bergen-Belsen (Dld.), één dag
na de bevrijding aldaar.

Figures 20 and 21: Me, on left, as baker's assistant to *Meneer* van Elewout, on right. The prayer card, made from Henk van Elewout's passport picture, explains that he died at the Bergen-Belsen concentration camp one day after it was liberated by allied forces. His final day of restored freedom took place on his 39th birthday.

Being twelve, I did not yet know what I wanted to be. I did mention to *Meneer* van Elewout that perhaps I, too, wanted to be a baker of cakes when I grew up. That comment did not fall upon deaf ears, and he suggested that I come and help him out after school to begin learning something of the confectioner trade.

He had little work to do; with the strict rationing and distributing of goods, it was difficult to get even basic ingredients such as butter, sugar, and flour. Anyone who ordered anything from his shop gave him certain ration cards in trade or brought in a specific amount of sugar or butter. Customers came into the shop, for example, with half a package of butter. Van Elewout then cut off a chuck of butter, sufficient for what the customer wanted him to make. That butter slice was then added to a large mound of accumulating chunks.

The first week I was only allowed to roll out *borstplaat*. Later, I was told to keep an eye on the clock to see when the *Jan Hagel*, a type of cookie, should be taken out of the oven. Still later, I was allowed to press cookies out of the dough using a cutter.

While looking for the right cookie cutter, I found a piece of dried old bread as white as snow and as hard as a rock. I just could not believe how white it was! The only bread I knew was so much duller—almost grey. "Was bread once really this white?" I asked him. Van Elewout answered: "Yes, Jan, it was just that white, only softer."

Baker van Elewout would wait for me to arrive to begin the work, because otherwise it would all be finished before I came to help; that's how little work there was during the war. Once in a while, he would even say: 'Jan, better not come tomorrow. I'll see you next week.'

That Meneer van Elewout stood on 'the right side' of things was obvious. He even sold little tiles with rhyming text:

> 'Learn from the wee fish under water,
> Splash about but hold your natter.'

I recall that the little fish on his tiles was orange and it swam in waves of red, white, and blue. The profits of the tiles were intended for the support of the underground resistance, or *De Ondergrondse*.

Figure 22: 1944 Resistance tile in the collection of the Museum of Rotterdam (item number 40686).

One day he left me alone in the bakery so that he might say goodbye in the vestibule to his girlfriend, who occasionally dropped by. When, after what seemed like a long time to me, they had finally left off saying goodbye and she was gone, he asked: 'Don't you think she's splendid?' I did not answer. She never even spoke to me, so why would I think her so wonderful? But he, in any case, clearly thought her tremendous.

One afternoon after school, I arrived at the bakery but found the shop door locked. Because Meneer van Elewout had not mentioned anything to me about not needing to come, I banged hard on the door a few times. After a long delay, the door was opened by a man whom I did not recognize. He did not let me in but said, 'You're Jan, right? Best go home. Meneer van Elewout has been picked up. You better leave quickly,' whereupon he closed the door again.

Our own house was scarce 100 meters from the shop, so within a few minutes I was home telling my father about what had just happened. He immediately asked: 'Did you recognize the man who opened the door?' I shook my head 'no,' and he followed up in his strictest tone: 'I absolutely forbid you to return there, and from now on you are to stay out of that shop.'

I then told my father that I knew where an illegal radio was hidden in the bakery basement. I also told him about the illegal newspapers and tiles that were under the shop's counter—and how those tiles were sold to support the resistance. That's when my father asked, 'Do you know where the parents of Meneer van Elewout live?' Now, that I knew, so he added: 'Well, then you may go there to tell them what you know.'

That is exactly what happened next. Once arrived at their house, I told them my tale. The man who had spoken to me at the bakery door proved the brother of Meneer van Elewout. His sister, also, was there. She thanked me for coming. She told me that she would walk over to the shop with a baby carriage to remove the radio, illegal newspapers, and tiles.

About ten days later, I heard that Meneer van Elewout had been taken to Germany via camp Vught. In the train, he managed to pass a note to a fellow traveler with the request to send it home. The final line in that note was supposedly 'And give my best to Jan.' When I heard that last bit, I wondered whether the story was really true, or whether I was kindly being told something that was made up—as a soothing gesture. My doubt about the anecdote never left me as the question could never be asked, since Meneer van Elewout never came back!

These events made a deep impression upon me. Because of what had happened, I added to my nightly prayers a section written especially for the return of all prisoners. Quickly, I learned it by heart, repeating it during mass on Sundays too.

Six months or so later, the school's doctor visited—and with him a nurse who assisted him in his check ups. Perhaps I was still so caught up in the drama of Meneer van Elewout, but I thought her the spitting image of the baker's girlfriend. I was taken aback by her appearance, debating with myself whether I should approach her, just to say, 'He loved you.' Because I did not know who had betrayed Meneer van Elewout, it might even have been the girlfriend, making her a 'suspect.'

Because of that uncertainty, I did not dare say anything to her.

After the war, I heard from a Meneer Rust, a friend of Meneer van Elewout, what happened on the fatal day of his forced disappearance. That very day there was, according to this man, a scheduled meeting of a group among the resistance. After the meeting, the first person to leave the shop was quietly arrested by the Germans on the corner of the street. Ten minutes later, the next member of the group left the shop, only to be picked up in the same way. In this manner, everyone in the group was picked off, one by one.

Later, is was discovered that someone living in one of the apartments above the bakery had informed the Germans that a lot of young people often entered the shop, staying sometimes for hours. That information alone had been enough to arrest the whole group and deport them.

I always regretted not having had the nerve to address that school nurse. Whether she indeed was the girlfriend of Meneer van Elewout, I shall therefore never know. But I am deeply saddened that she never received, via a small boy, an affirmation of his regard for her. I shall always regret that my fears about addressing her won out over my desire to tell her something good and beautiful.

41

Figure 23a and b: Monument in memory of the fallen members of the local Dutch resistance along the Prins Bernhardlaan in Voorburg.

Chapter 10
As the occupiers turned up the pressure, so did the resistance

We were now three years into the war. Although I had not understood at the start why we resisted the Germans so little, the reasons were becoming clearer every day; the resistance was occurring 'under ground.' The Germans reacted harshly to anything that did not please them. For example, I had heard, even when we still lived in the Vogelwijk, about the 'February strike' that took place in Amsterdam in 1941. People there had, in protest against the forced removal of the Jews, walked away from their work.

The trams stopped and the conductors refused to move them along. Factory workers stopped their work and filled the streets to give voice to their anger. The Germans answered by executing eight innocent people. Information about the execution was broadly disseminated via radio, handbills, and posters; we did not yet have television in those days.

This is why I perfectly understood what my father meant when he reacted to the news that the American marine base in Pearl Harbor had been bombed by the Japanese. 'Thank goodness,' he had sighed. Now, he explained, we are no longer alone, because America is pulled into the war. We were going to receive help, even if it would take time— just how long we did not yet realise.

From the first days of the war, the Dutch government instituted mandatory 'blackouts'. It was your responsibility to make sure that the lights inside your home were not visible from the street, by hanging heavy curtains or placing blackout paper on the windows. Naturally there were no streetlights! The Germans now took over this measure, expanding the prohibition to include lights on all vehicles, even bicycles. Headlights had to be covered with black material, leaving only a small horizontal stripe of less than one centimeter thickness that could be illuminated.

At one point the Germans added a *samenscholingsverbod*, which meant that groups of four people or more were not allowed to stand together in the street. The Germans announced their right to shoot, without warning, any persons who did not follow this directive. Furthermore, it was declared illegal to listen to British radio broadcasts. If you did tune in, and you were caught, you risked severe punishments—possibly even execution. This prohibition was so widely ignored, and this in spite of the severity of the likely punishment, that the Germans eventually decided to confiscate all radios. I still recall how my father practically threw his radio on the back of his bicycle in disgust, before turning it in at the local school occupied by German soldiers.

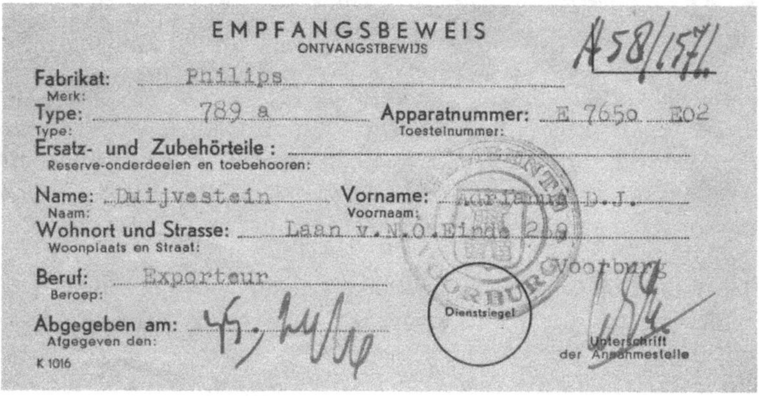

Figure 24: The 'receipt' for our confiscated radio.

Newspapers were heavily censored, so that we could only read how the Germans viewed the progress of the war. This is why underground newspapers came into being. These were printed in secret.

There were a number of well-meaning Dutch citizens who sent their kids, of about ten years of age, to distribute these clandestine papers. I found it unthinkable that parents exposed their own children needlessly to that level of risk. To think that illegal printers often carried an identification certificate with them that read: 'The holder of these papers belongs to the illegal underground and has the right to access the presses.' I saw such an ID myself once and suspected its owner of wanting to impress others with his bravery. If the Germans found such papers during an inspection, an execution would be sure to follow.

Such fanaticism and extreme confidence stood in stark contrast to what happened to these newspapers in our own house. We were taught never to take any unnecessary risks. In our house an illegal newspaper was gratefully read but then was made to disappear as quickly as possible. There was an underground paper that you could subscribe to, but my father definitely did not want to be on any subscription list.

Sometimes, when we sat around the table at dinner, the neighbour would tap on the wall with something hard. That meant: 'There is news.' 'Jan', my father would say, 'Meneer Peeting has news,' and I would climb the stairs to the second floor, where just at the back of our house, lay the bedroom of my parents. I had been instructed never to do this with the light on. So, in complete darkness, I would feel my way to the French doors of the small back balcony and open them. At the same time, I would hear the balcony doors at the neighbour open. 'Well, Jan, here is more good news,' our neighbour would usually whisper, while he looked round to see if we could be spotted by any other neighbours.

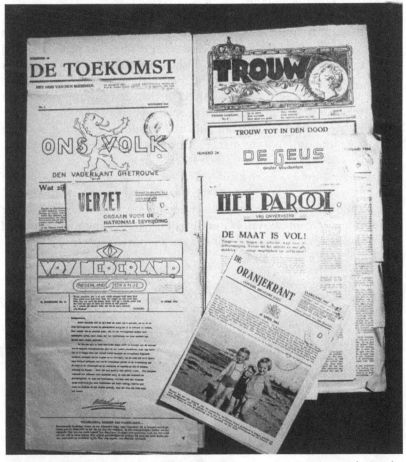

Figure 25: Surviving examples of illegal newspapers promoting resistance during the war. Beeldbank WO2 – NIOD (98027).

Meneer Peeting did not have any children of his own and after fifty years of marriage was presumably running low on conversational material with his wife. In any case, he would usually try to strike up a chat. Having to stand in the cold and the dark while whispering never made me all that eager to linger on the balcony. Downstairs it was, after all, cozy and warm. That's why I would usually keep to 'Thank you, Meneer Peeting, and please do say hello to your wife', while taking from his hand the illegal paper called *Vrij Nederland*, or *Free Holland*.

Upon my return downstairs, my father would invariably remark: 'You were gone a very long time.' This was because he feared that I might be seen by other neighbours.

After dinner, my father would sit in 'the big chair', an easy chair that was more or less reserved especially for him. After reading the paper, it would be torn into tiny little pieces and flushed down the toilet, in express violation of the request printed at the foot of the paper to 'multiply and distribute'. I remember being annoyed at this. Passing on good news was surely a positive thing for other people, especially in an increasingly difficulty time. Eventually I came to understand that my father didn't want to expose us to possible dangers through the carelessness of others.

It was at this same time that the *P.T.T.* office put out a special type of radio. It was a small box speaker that then received only two stations. It was called the *radiodistributie* and I remember just how perfectly clear and strong its reception was. Naturally, all programming was controlled by the Germans, and it could not receive any foreign news stations.

Figure 26: Simple radio box from the PTT, distributor of radio programmes. Displayed at Nederlands Openluchtmuseum, Arnhem.

On the 11th of April 1944, my father stood in our small back garden looking at the sky. I walked over to him and likewise looked up. He said: 'They have bombed Villa Kleykamp. Do you know what that means?' No, I had no idea. He explained that this building was where the population registry and many public records were stored.

At the request of the underground, the British had bombed a specific building along the Scheveningseweg—right across from *Het Vredespaleis*, or The Peace Palace. The absence of such records would then make it harder for the Germans to identify and pick up Dutch citizens. My father said that the English pilot managed to hit only that one building, leaving everything around it standing.

'And do you know why they bombed it during the lunch hour?' he continued. Without waiting for my answer, he added, 'Because that's when there are the fewest people inside the building.' Regardless, there were still 60 casualties. Rumour had it that most of those killed were N.S.B-ers. Once again, I was stunned that my father knew the details of a British bombardment barely an hour after it had occurred.

Chapter 11
Fietsenrazzias

The street scene changed radically in the years 1943 and '44. With rare exception, you did not see cars on the street anymore. Exceptions were cars with Germans behind the wheel.

With cars scarce, our occupiers became increasingly interested in bicycles—our bicycles, or *fietsen*. To avoid having one's *fiets* confiscated, folks thought up all sorts of 'tricks'. Some lengthened the front fork and mounted there a small scooter wheel. Tires were swapped out for pieces of garden hose. To ride a bike with hoses for tires was uncomfortable. Every turn of the wheel became a small attack on the kidneys. The Germans were not interested in any such altered or doctored bikes, but they were very keen on 'normal' cycles in working order.

Concealed flatbed trucks with a few German soldiers with racing bikes beside them became a routine sight along roads. Many a Dutchman biked right into such a hidden roadblock and was forced to surrender his bicycle.

Figure 27: Confiscated bicycles were carted away on open trucks or horse-drawn carts. Beeldbank WO2 – NIOD (83309).

On the street, whenever a fellow patriot whispered, 'Watch out, *fietsenrazzia!*' then you knew to gratefully turn around and make yourself scarce. Even such a well-meant warning was not without some element of risk, since a German sympathiser might turn that person in for giving the game away. Such a warning also had to occur out of sight and earshot of any Germans.

So it did happen that German soldiers with racing bikes, and binoculars around their necks, would occasionally spot a cyclist heading their way and witness him turn around quite suddenly in the opposite direction. Then they would pursue him at top speed. Any nearby observers would hold their breath, although the person fleeing would usually get overtaken. It was often an unfair race, since an older person, scared and physically weak, could be no match for a fit and well-fed young soldier.

It was clear why the Germans dared to let passersby gather to witness their bike catches, thus allowing us to violate their own prohibition against even small groupings of people. As their trucks filled with bikes, the Germans continued until they could triumphantly depart with a full demoralising load.

It is unnecessary to explain just how much any spectator enjoyed the sight of a soldier heading off to overtake a fleeing cyclist only to return fifteen minutes later, alone and sweaty from effort. This meant a bike had managed to get away. Although spectators remained po-faced because they could not signal their delight, God saw all, and He saw that is was good. Witnesses also remained steadfastly silent, because giving an opinion or making a comment could be dangerous too.

This is why I was so surprised when a total stranger addressed me in such a roadside group. 'Do you have a moment?' he asked, while moving away from the others. Once we were at a little distance from the rest, he told me that his bike now stood on one of those trucks. He wanted to try to get his bike back. He did not, however, want to take his bag with him while making the attempt. So he asked me, 'Could you put my bag in a safe place for me for a little while.'

I didn't think that was a problem, so I led him to my house, which was nearby. The man waited outside, while I climbed two sets of stairs to hide his bag in the hatch inside my own bedroom. Once back on the street we returned to the truck, where the man spoke to the German soldiers. After a mere fifteen minutes he returned, disappointed and unsuccessful. He'd not be able to talk them into giving him back his bike.

Together we walked back to my house, where we picked his bag up again. He opened the bag in front of me and I saw that it was full of packages of cigarettes. He gave me one, thanked me, and left.

The cigarettes were entirely unmarked, without any printing on the blank paper packaging. That meant these brandless cigarettes were made from homegrown tobacco.

That same day I received from Adriaan de Veer, a man who worked for my father, a bid of 25 guilders for my package of unbranded, homemade cigarettes. That made for a quick sale. The next day I was told that he had already resold it for double that amount. Before the war, such a package of low-quality homemade cigarettes would have been deemed worthless.

Chapter 12
Scarcity makes for creativity

Times were getting increasingly tough. Money became less and less valuable. If something broke and needed a new part, you might as well forget about any repair. Replacement parts were simply not available. Clothing too was scarcely for sale anywhere, so that the making of dresses, coats, and such became a coveted skill.

At about this time, my mother heard through the family Lijnkamp of a seamstress who might be able to make me a new coat. A few weeks later, a coat made from a blanket and paid for with Belgian endive hung in my closet, awaiting the coming of winter. That winter would be an extremely cold one and would go down in the history books as 'The Hunger Winter'.

I wore that coat a lot, sometimes with shiny patent leather shoes! Those shoes came from a so-called sailor choir, a boy's choir by the name of *Haags Matrozenkoor*. The founder and director was Meneer van Elferent, who also gave singing lessons at our school. Once, when he was told to perform for the Germans, he refused. A record was played instead, to give the impression that his boys were singing in the studio.

He also needed to eat, and in despondency offered the choir's uniforms and shiny patent-leather shoes in exchange for food. My mother saw a use for those shoes but, luckily, did not take to the little sailor suits. No one ever commented on my odd choice of outfit, one that combined a rough coat made from an old blanket with shiny dress shoes.

At that time, my father walked passed an almost-empty store window, in which lay a single hammer on display. He did not need one but thought, 'The day will come when there are no tools at all for sale anywhere, so I better go in and enquire'. He entered the store, heard that the hammer was indeed for sale, and purchased it.

Our local cobbler had gone into hiding after refusing to work for the Germans. A new shoe repairer had to be found. Via a tip from a friend, my father found another cobbler, one completely on the other side of town. This cobbler had plenty of work and was not exactly looking for a new client.

My father began: 'Sir, one day the war will be over. I promise you that if you help me now, we will remain your client even after the war'. To keep on the cobbler's good side, my father never even asked him about his prices for repairs. 'I will provide my own leather', added my father. Such a promise meant buying leather on the 'black market' for a rather large sum. The cobbler gave in to my father's pleas and a few weeks later I was allowed to bring him our shoes, so that he could professionally replace the soles and heels.

To make the shoes last longer, they were reinforced on the heels and soles with little iron nails and fittings, called hobnails. The hobnails made a clicking sound when walking that I thought rather cool—like a soldier. Even so, I did understand why other people asked us to take off such shoes when visiting.

My father dutifully followed up on his promise to remain loyal to that cobbler after the war. Even though his shop was clear on the other side of town, we remained one of his best clients until his death, and I was still often sent there on errands. When there was the rare exception, as in the case of new heels for a delicate pair of ladies shoes, my mother would whisper 'Don't tell your father, but best just drop these at the nearby cobbler'. When our war-time cobbler retired to a small flat in Mariahoeve, he said: 'I'm cancelling all of my clients except my very best. That includes your family, of course'.

Chapter 13
The Hunger Winter approaches

In the autumn of 1944 my father decided to make special arrangements to make it through the winter. Food prices had risen enormously. Although rumours were spreading that the war would soon come to an end, my father wanted some insurance for the months ahead. He approached an acquaintance, Meneer Stout, with a proposition.

Meneer Stout was, before the war, the representative of a large wholesaler in cheese and eggs, or *kaas en eieren*. In addition to making his weekly rounds among retailers, he also visited a few private clients, with an eye to increasing his sales. Among them were a number of large families, including ours. During the initial years of the war he had continued to come to our door regularly with his wares and advice.

He had also signaled to us that he remained 'on the side of good', which was important if you wanted to continue to do business. The sale of wares outside of German-sanctioned rules was, after all, strictly forbidden and punishable with jail time and even execution. Some time earlier, the occupiers had instituted a coupon system. In practice, this meant that there was an announcement every month identifying which numbered ration coupons could be used for foods such as bread, cheese, sugar, butter, and even candy.

The Germans monitored all activity closely, making sure that only those foods regulated by their coupon system were available. Even so, everyone tried, often unsuccessfully, to somehow find more to eat. The so-called 'black market', the secret and illegal trading of goods that no one could see and therefore took place in the 'dark', was forbidden.

Even petty thefts born out of desperation or hunger were severely punished. One boy, who had been caught stealing a piece of fruit from a grocer in Den Haag, was forced to stand in front of the shop while holding up a piece of cardboard. On the cardboard was written: 'I am a plunderer'. After having stood that way for hours, the boy was shot dead. His body, with upon it the cardboard sign, was placed in the shop window as a deterrent to others.

Figure 28: Customers needed ration coupons in order to purchase food. Beeldbank WO2 – NIOD (82453).

Horror stories of events like this spread like wildfire. While that boy still lived and stood in front of that shop, I heard about him even though I lived in Voorburg and this gruesome incident took place in central Den Haag. I thought to myself, 'I'm not going there to watch that'. Soon after I found out he had been killed. By means of such stories, fear grew strong and deep and people found less and less courage to resist the Germans, opting to obediently follow the rules instead.

It was at this moment and in this context that my father approached Meneer Stout with his proposition. My father told him how he owned a house in the Carpentierstraat, at number 14. The substantial building, which consisted of four floors, was leased to a woman who ran a small business there renting out rooms. He wanted to sell this building, not for money, but for staples such as wheat and potatoes.

He needed to find a farmer or grower who was open to such a transaction and who was not only trustworthy but could arrange for transport. This was a tall order and the reason why my father had approached Meneer Stout, whose business might have put him in touch with various farmers and suppliers.

A few days later, my father met again with Meneer Stout who had, to avoid unnecessary risk, approached a brother-in-law who owned a farm in Zoetermeer. His brother-in-law looked with a favorable eye upon a transaction such as this. A week later this trio gathered to share the pleasure of a pre-war cigar, supplied by my father, and discuss the details of the proposed deal. The number of sacks of wheat and potatoes, as well as the manner of delivery, was agreed upon.

In order to avoid the Germans catching wind of such an arrangement, it was decided not to transfer the deed to the property. The building would remain in my father's name. Only after the war was over would the all-important legal transfer of the property take place.

A few weeks later, a horse and cart stopped in front of our house in darkness. At that hour it was *spertijd* and strictly forbidden to be outside on the street. At first glance, the cart looked to be carrying only sugar beets, but underneath them lay sacks of potatoes and wheat. The whole family was waiting in the hallway to speedily unload the wagon and, soundlessly and without any light, heave the sacks inside.

The blanket of sugar beets that had cloaked our secret load remained behind in the cart. While my mother furnished the driver with a cup of coffee, my father distributed the sacks. In less than fifteen minutes, all the sacks of potatoes were down in the cellar and the wheat up on the first floor. The driver was already off with his load of sugar beets. If he lingered too long, a cart with sugar beets stopped after dark in front of a house in a residential neighbourhood might otherwise attract attention.

About ten days later, the exact same scene was repeated, and for the final time. While my father doled out the heavy sacks, the driver told my mother of how, along the way, some folks had snagged a few of the sugar beets and had nearly discovered the sacks underneath. My mother praised him by saying, 'I think it quite wonderful how you arranged to bring everything to us so rapidly'. The driver remained silent.

My father later told us that the man was a member of the N.S.B. and cooperated with the Germans. He apparently belonged with those who had joined the side of the Germans but, as the war grew to a close, wanted some insurance from the other side. Later, would he own up to having been in the wrong but claim that he had also done a few good things?

Was the end of the war really in sight? After all, only a few months earlier there had been a failed attempt to assassinate Hitler. Stories circulated that the allies were on their way, and that brought hope.

When, on Tuesday 5 September 1944, we saw a convoy of German vehicles leave, we too began to believe in those stories. There were even a few people who dared to hang out the Dutch flag in celebration. But the elation lasted only a short while, and later that evening we already knew better. *Dolle Dinsdag*, or 'Mad Tuesday', was over. The streetlights were out. Not a soul on the street and no traffic of any sort. Everything seemed scarily quiet, like a calm before a storm. The very worst was yet to come.

After the war, my father paid a visit to the farmer, Meneer Stout's brother-in-law, in order to fulfill his pledge to legally transfer title of the property to him. The farmer expressed his intention to simply sell the building. My father, in turn, said he was willing to buy it back. The parties soon reached a financial agreement that put aside any need for transfer paperwork. My father retained possession.

Chapter 14
Our land divided between liberated and occupied

Starting in September of 1944, our country was only partially made free. After landing at Normandy on the 6th of June, the allies had fought steadily to eventually reach, just beyond Belgium, the border of Holland.

Even though it was strictly forbidden to listen to the British radio station (to the limited extent that this was even possible after the requisition of radios), everyone somehow knew exactly how far the allied forces had progressed. We knew that the Dutch province of Limburg was free, but that the crossing of the big rivers in the middle of Holland had, in the face of heavy opposition from the German troops, slowed progress.

Although many German soldiers had been pulled away to the front lines, in the west of the country we still saw plenty. A few weeks earlier, on *Dolle Dinsdag*, we'd thought that the end was in sight, but now we realised that it had been a false celebration, started by rumours of approaching allied soldiers. A few people even swore to have seen our liberators. The headlong departure of some families who had sympathised with the Germans was enough to make us all believe in imminent freedom. That night, the end of *Dolle Dinsdag*, we'd not only felt disappointment but surprise at how mere rumours could have generated our false sense of euphoria.

Figure 29: With my friend Ben Pas, dressed as bride and groom at the roller skating race in de Eerste van de Boschstraat sometime in 1944. I am the bride.

The absence of traffic and the closing of schools prompted neighbourhoods to hold street fairs and dress-up contests—a rare diversion for us kids. Dressed up as a bride, with my friend Ben Pas as the groom, I participated in one of the roller skating contests that drew spectators along the 1ste van de Boschstraat in the Bezuidenhout neighbourhood. Most spectators, you can see from the photo, were children.

Figures 30a and b: Ben and I in faux Indonesian costume, and between us *Mina Bakgraag*. Also in that first photo, my brother Adri is visible behind my left shoulder, although not in costume. On the back of one of the photos, my mother recorded the date as 29 October 1944. The homes visible in the group photo confirm the location as the Laan van Nieuw Oost-Indië.

In the next such contest, another pal of ours, cross-dressed as *Mina Bakgraag* in a giant wig and with a thick pair of gloves padding both his front and backsides, scooped up first place. By then we'd changed our bridal outfits for Indonesian-style jackets. Ben and I, in our matching costumes, received a prize too, namely a *Kwartetspel* that betrayed signs of having been previously played. We didn't care about any of that.

Schools closed because of a lack of heating; there was no more coal. Although I was a kid who eagerly looked forward to any and all school vacations, I remember not being at all enthusiastic about this new development. Things were different now.

On the last school day our class had just celebrated the birthday of our teacher. I brought my present for her in an envelope: two spoonfuls of tea for a wartime cuppa. 'Come Sunday, I'm really going to enjoy this', she had told me. 'I'm delighted with this gift'. I knew that she meant it too, because real tea had not been for sale for a few years now. 'This is the best present of all', I had thought too great an honour.

School let out at four o'clock. When we walked past the church along the Schenkkade we saw a tall crane with a group of boys nearby. Because all building construction had stopped years earlier, a big crane like this struck us all of us as worth watching. What we saw was hard to comprehend.

The church bells, <u>our</u> church bells from the *Liduinakerk*, were being hoisted out of their spire. Two smaller bells had already been removed and stood on the ground awaiting transport. In order to remove the larger third, the sound hole of the bell tower had to be widened. It was a fascinating mechanical spectacle, until we began to realise what was really happening.

The Germans were removing our church bells in order to melt them down and turn them into bullets! I again marveled at the resignation that would allow this. The inscription *Laudate Dominum* was legible on one of the bells. One of the witnesses knew enough Latin to translate this into 'Praise Our Lord God'. His translation seamlessly connected with my thoughts at that moment: well, at least the text did not refer to these *moffen*. You'd have to have a pretty high opinion of yourself to go so far as to steal the bells of a church in order to turn them into bullets. Although it was unbelievable, it was nonetheless true.

On Sunday I wondered why that day's sermon did not make clear how anyone who had taken part in the removal of the bells would burn in hell. To me this seemed like such a reasonable punishment. But nothing like that edict was issued from the pulpit.

Chapter 15
My mother's scariest day

In November of 1944 there was yet another directive from the occupiers to the effect that every able-bodied man between seventeen and forty, inclusive, had to report to the authorities. Before that, starting in May 1943, the order had sounded only for men of eighteen to thirty-five. Thus the age was lowered at the front end and extended at the back. Even with the threat that those refusing would be shot on sight, the order to turn oneself in would not yield a lot of volunteers. Anyone who did obey was immediately transported to Germany where they were forced to labor in the German war machine. Because factories producing weaponry were regularly bombed by allied forces, it was best to avoid such places. My father saved the paper order, or *bevel*, noting even the hour and date of receipt: 21 November 1944 at 7:30 am. That was just five weeks shy of his 41st birthday on 28 December. The order arrived when my father was ill, and he spent the next five weeks in bed upstairs, wearing his pajamas, just in case the Germans came to search the house.

BEVEL. *21, 11, 44 7:30*

Op bevel der **Duitsche Weermacht** moeten alle mannen in den leeftijd van 17 t/m 40 jaar zich voor den arbeidsinzet aanmelden.

Hiervoor moeten **ALLE** mannen van dezen leeftijd onmiddellijk na ontvangst van dit bevel met de voorgeschreven uitrusting op straat gaan staan.

Alle andere bewoners, ook vrouwen en kinderen, moeten in de huizen blijven totdat de actie ten einde is. De mannen van de genoemde jaargangen, die bij een huiszoeking nog in huis worden aangetroffen, worden gestraft, waarbij hun particulier eigendom zal worden aangesproken.

Bewijzen van vrijstelling van burgerlijke of militaire instanties moeten ter contrôle worden meegebracht. Ook zij, die in het bezit zijn van zulke bewijzen, zijn verplicht zich op straat te begeven.

Er moeten worden medegebracht: warme kleeding, stevige schoenen, dekens, bescherming tegen regen, eetgerei, mes, vork, lepel, drinkbeker en boterhammen voor één dag.

De **dagelijksche vergoeding bestaat uit goeden kost, rookartikelen en loon volgens het geldende tarief.** Voor de **achterblijvende familieleden zal worden gezorgd.**

Het is aan alle bewoners der gemeente verboden hun woonplaats te verlaten.

Op hen, die pogen te ontvluchten of weerstand te bieden, zal worden geschoten.

Figure 31: My father's copy of the German *BEVEL*, or order, for all men ages 17 through 40 (inclusive) to appear in readiness on the street, supplied with 'warm clothing, walking shoes, blankets, rain gear, utensils, cup and sandwiches for one day'. It ends with the warning not to leave one's home and that 'those who attempt to flee or offer resistance will be shot'.

To gather men who had not reported in voluntarily, the Germans regularly conducted *razzias*, or raids. Secret hiding places were created for concealment during times of danger. Ceilings were lowered and false walls inserted, so that men might have spaces to hide in, if needed. Alterations of this sort had to occur silently and without any talk. A story circulated that a handyman in Haarlem had performed upwards of eighty little alterations like this, without his own wife even knowing anything about it.

During this same period, towards the close of 1944 but before 21 November because it occurred on a day that my father was out of the house, something significant happened that stayed with me—and also with my mother.

One day, when my mother, our maid Annie, and I were the only people home in our house on the Laan van Nieuw Oosteinde, we were astonished to see, looking through the window, that our street was being blocked off for a stretch of about 150 meters. On either side, the road was now barred by two German trucks, each filled with about thirty German soldiers seated back-to back on wooden benches with rifles slung around their necks.

When our maid saw this she asked my mother, 'Ma'am, can I go home? I don't feel so well'. 'You go, Annie', said my mother. And within seconds Annie was gone, out onto the street.

For better and less conspicuous viewing of what was going on outside, my mother and I went to the top floor of the house—to the bedroom that I shared with my brother Kees. After all, we had nothing to fear. Not only did we not have anyone in hiding but no one in our family at the moment fell within the age group that was being called up for forced labor. We nonetheless became frightened when we realised the true reason for the blocking off of our street: this was a *fietsenrazzia*, aimed at the collection of bikes.

The Germans rang the bell at every house, and as soon as the front door opened they entered without a word of apology. Every few houses or so they came out with a bike. The confiscated bicycles were placed onto one of the trucks for removal. My mother asked anxiously, 'Jan, what shall we do now?'

We were in a bit of a pickle. Less than a week earlier, at the dinner

64

table, it had been decided to hide away the family's three remaining bicycles. Two of the bikes were now in my and Kees' bedroom, which was on the second floor, while the third bike was in my father's study on the first floor. As I did not answer my mother's rhetorical question, she followed it up with 'We're just not going to open the door'.

When the army trucks approached nearer to our own house, we moved away from the window and anxiously sat on the edge of my bed. Soon, we heard a forceful ringing of our front door bell. 'I'm really not going to answer that', said my mother, as if I were in any doubt. The bell rang again and in a manner that suggested the German soldiers fully intended to come inside.

After about ten minutes we relaxed, thinking that we'd escaped the search patrol, until we heard heavy footfalls on the floor below— coming from inside the house.

'Ist jemand da?' someone called in German.

'Jan, they are inside', whispered my mother with fear in her voice. She added: 'Get undressed and crawl into bed. I'm going downstairs'.

Left behind, I was now alone in my room. I broke into a sweat from the fear, asking myself how in heaven's name they'd managed to come inside. I was staring straight at the two bikes, less than two meters from my bed. The plan had been to dismantle them and store the parts under the roof.

I wondered what was happening downstairs. My fearful thoughts were interrupted by the muffled sounds of the German soldier climbing the stairs. My mother, in Annie's role as housemaid, warned him in schoolgirl German not to enter my room because I was sick: 'Betreten Sie nicht das Zimmer, in dem ihr kranker Sohn schläft.' Without comment, he skipped my room. After looking into those of my brothers and sisters next door, he walked downstairs again.

I did not dare leave my bed and so could only wait, full of fear and anxiety for my mother's return. Finally, she came. She had to take a moment to collect herself, but then out came the story...

The German soldier who rang our doorbell without getting a response had then 'honoured' our neighbours with a visit. The couple next door were in their seventies and had neither children nor bicycles. Via their balcony on the first floor at the back, the soldier had been able to climb onto our own balcony, something that was not hard for a young man to manage. From there he'd simply entered via the French doors, which had stood slightly ajar, held by only a little hook to air out the house.

As she told the story, my mother had hailed him with a friendly greeting, telling him that she was the maid. 'Ich bin die Hilfe und nicht erlaubt die Tür zu öffnen', she had told him politely in German. The soldier had interrupted her with a question about the presence of bicycles: 'Haben Sie Fahrräder?' 'Nein, wir haben kein Fahrräder', she had managed to answer over her pounding heart.

The soldier then wandered into various rooms, after which he walked downstairs to locate the basement. 'Sie haben doch Fahrräder', was his conclusion when he walked back up the basement stairs. None of us had thought about the tire pump when it had been decided to hide the bicycles. That oversight now created a problem, for he'd found the pump in the basement.

'Ja, ja wir haben ein Fahrrad', admitted my mother slyly, as the soldier followed her submissively to the garden and the shed. There, she pointed to a small children's bike that stood in the shed's corner with two pathetically flat tires. 'Das meine ich nicht', said the frustrated German.

Without another word, he walked to the front door. Just as he was about to open it, my father arrived home. My mother, sticking to her part as the hired help, addressed him formally with 'Guten Tag, Herr Duijvestein. Ich habe gesagt das Ich nicht erlaubt war, die Tür zu öffnen'.

'Was ist hier los?' asked my father, also in fine German, a language which he had mastered before the war as part of his job, which was the importing and exporting of fruits and vegetables. The German soldier then demanded whether he was in possession of a bicycle.

Without answering, my father reached for his wallet, from which he produced a letter with at least five official-looking seals and stamps and offered it as if a real permit to keep a bicycle. 'Bitte, ich bin erlaubt ein Fahrräd zu haben', he said. 'Von woher kommen Sie?' he asked casually. 'Aus Dortmund', said the young man, while handing back the paper.

Perhaps emboldened by the fact that the German did not recognize the document as a fake permit, or inspired by the adage that the best defense is a good offense, my father continued with something along the lines of 'Once this war is over, my German clients shall not believe what has transpired here during the occupation'. The soldier decided not to hear the rest of this story and left the house.

My mother and I watched his departure from the top floor. Afterwards, we quickly descended the stairs to discuss the day's bizarre events—the three of us sitting conspiratorially around the table. Only that evening, when regaling the others with our story, did we realise that the soldier also had not noticed the bike on the first floor. It was leaning against the wall just behind the door of my father's study, which would have been apparent to anyone who had peered around the study door.

Flash forward to about 1990. A generous forty years after the war, my mother and I are sharing stories over a cup of coffee. 'Jan, do you know what I thought the scariest day in my life? The day that we were home alone and the Germans held their fietsenrazzia. *I was so frightened'. I, for one, utterly understood her fear.*

Chapter 16
'Our' bicycle lamps

Six months or so before the war came to an end it was increasingly difficult to find food. Long lines formed before shops and soup kitchens—places where anyone might wait in line for a gratis meal. Whether you needed ration tickets for those kitchens, I never knew. Luckily, our family never had to avail themselves of the soup kitchens, because thanks to my father's efforts we still had things to eat.

Every night at half past six, a regular guest rang our doorbell. I would walk to the front door via the kitchen, where I would pick up a chair for him. With the chair already in one hand, I would open the door with the other.

That this young man, the eldest son of a large family in our parish, had to eat his meal all alone in the front hallway, I thought a little sad. But when, after half an hour, I came to retrieve his plate, I would find that his appetite has not suffered from the solitude. The plate would be licked clean and the guest gone.

When I returned to the dining room to join the others at table, the conversation would resume at its natural volume. While our 'guest' remained in the hall, discussion occurred in hushed tones, a fact that I considered perfectly normal.

One day, when I opened the front door for him, he said: 'May I please ask your mother a question?' The young man informed her that he would soon be turning seventeen and intended to go into hiding. He wanted to know if his brother might then take his place. To his great relief, there was no objection.

Although we still had food every day, the menu was monotonous. My mother also decided no longer to peel the potatoes because, as she explained, the most nutritious part of the potato was right under the skin.

Even potatoes were getting scarce and costly. As a result, it became increasingly common for the doorbell to be rung by someone asking,

'Could you perhaps spare one potato?' If you gave such a person a potato, you would run the risk of having another family member ring your bell an hour later.

Food became such a scarce commodity that you had to be increasingly sparing and careful. This is the context in which a story took place that my mother told after the war.

One day she was busy cooking a meal on the *kolenkachel* in the living room when the cooking pot fell over, spreading all of the vegetables in a mess on the carpet. As it happened, the priest from the Luduinakerk was just then paying a visit. Seeing the doubt flash over my mother's face, he said, 'Woman, just toss it back in the pot. No one will be the wiser'. Food was precious.

Other things that became scarce included gas, water, and electricity. Gas and electricity were soon only available during certain hours. Outside of those set times supplies were temporarily turned off by the utility company. This mattered less during the day, but at night the lack of electricity was a real inconvenience. Eventually, there was no electric power at all.

For a few months we made do with a carbide lamp. I liked how it smelled when you spat on the flame. Others just thought the carbide stank. After the carbide lamp we had an oil lamp. We even floated little cotton fuses in saucers of oil, which were then lit. All of this gave off relatively little light, so that we sat in a dusky darkness every evening.

We were therefore delighted when my father found a solution to this problem. One day he pulled a handful of bicycle lamps out of his pocket, each one connected to the other with thin electrical wire. The string of lamps and wire ended in an electrical plug.

We were amazed to see that when he stuck the plug in the outlet, quite a bit of good light emanated from the five low-voltage lights—enough even to read by. How was that possible? My father was only too pleased to explain.

Once the Germans had turned off the power completely, he'd been searching for another source of electricity. He knew the brother-in-law of his own brother Kees, who worked for the telephone services company, the P.T.T. In exchange for money and food, he helped people acquire a weak low-voltage electricity by changing over some wires and connections at the central office.

How exactly this worked, and whether the low-voltage power was extended via telephone or radio-wires, we were not told. But he had arranged it. Fantastic, we had power! In order to maintain control, my father decided to limit our use of such lights to the living room.

A few weeks later, Meneer Morshuis, a friend of my father's, walked unexpectedly straight into the living room. Surprised by the radiance of our bikelamp-lit living room, he shouted· 'What? You have light?' 'Sure, we have light', answered my father dryly. 'But how is that possible?' asked Meneer Morshuis.

'Well, I'll tell you, Henk. We were told that ever since the power was cut, low-voltage current continues to flow into some residences. As you see, that seems to be the case with us'. 'Could that be true at our place, too?' asked Meneer Morshuis, 'I don't know', said my father. 'But why don't you give it a try?' added my mother. After listening to an explanation of how to connect the bike lamps, he departed.

How Meneer Morshuis had managed to suddenly appear in the living room was explained by my brother Gerard, after his departure. Gerard had reached home just as Meneer Morshuis arrived. With his key already in hand to open the front door, Gerard had been asked 'Is your father at home?' When Gerard said that he did not know, Meneer Morshuis had simply accompanied him inside.

After a little while, Meneer Morshuis returned visibly disappointed, declaring 'Well, it doesn't work at our place. We tried every outlet'. 'How frustrating', sympathized my mother. 'We were told that it works for very very few', she cautioned. 'That's why we didn't mention anything before'. 'An incredible shame that it doesn't work for us', sighed Meneer Morshuis.

'It is nice… that light', mumbled Meneer Morshuis when, just before ten o'clock, he stood up from his chair. There was just enough time to reach his own dark house, which stood less than one hundred meters from our own. He had to be back home by ten, which was *spertijd*, or curfew, the time after which it became illegal to be out on the street.

Chapter 17
The miller in Nootdorp

The end of January 1945 was the heart of a hard winter. A thick layer of snow blanketed everything in white. With so little traffic, the landscape looked very picturesque.

After breakfast, my father asked me to come to his study on the first floor, for he wanted to ask me something. We were taught never to enter his study unless expressly invited. When you were asked to go there, you knew it was for an important reason. In this case, the importance was clear after about five minutes.

It concerned a few bags of wheat, the result of another transaction that had taken place a few months earlier. In order to turn the wheat into flour for baking the kernels had to be ground. During the previous weeks, all us kids had sat at the dining room table taking turns with the hand-cranked coffee mill between our knees.

The coffee mill was the only tool we had with which to grind the wheat into flour, but it made for an impossible job. Utterly frustrating! If, after turning the stiff handle of the mill for a quarter of an hour, you peeked into the little drawer on the bottom, it was hard to see any progress since the last time you looked.

'Jan, I think that I found a solution for this', announced my father. He told me that Meneer Kortekaas, an acquaintance, owned a windmill in Nootdorp. My father had mentioned to him our difficulty with the wheat and Meneer Kortekaas had suggested his tenant could help.

'What if you took your sled to the miller in Nootdorp today', proposed my father. 'I'll give you a bag of the wheat to take along. If you have that milled for us, our problem is solved.' A half an hour later, I was pulling my sled toward Nootdorp, which lay at a distance of about twelve kilometers.

My mother had promised to make *pannekoeken* for dinner, and to wait with eating them until I returned. While the *pannekoeken* made during the war were of lesser quality than those from before the war, I was still looking forward to this dinner treat. The fact that my mother had made me this special promise also gave me a fine feeling.

There were two ways to get to Nootdorp. I could walk along the Laan van Nieuw Oosteinde and take the viaduct over the Vliet or I could take the longer way along the Bilderdijklaan, which would add a good twenty minutes to the trip. I opted to take the longer route, so that I could avoid the German guard post at the end of the viaduct. After all, school was out for a whole month, so I had plenty of free time.

The large windmill was not hard to spot, and when I approached I had my story ready. 'I bring you best wishes from Meneer Kortekaas, who said that you would probably be able to help', I began.

After only about ten minutes, I was again en route towards home, pulling the milled bag of wheat on the sled behind me. I walked the same way back and reached home in about three hours. That night I felt pretty important when my mother announced that we were eating pancakes because of a special promise made to me.

A few weeks later, my father again asked me to walk with him upstairs. In his study he told me that as soon as I had returned from the mill with the ground wheat, he had put the bag on the scale. It weighed about half a kilo less than it did before I set out. He suspected that the miller had helped himself to that portion.

When you go again today, could you ask him the following: 'My father asks whether wheat tends to weigh less after it is milled into flour?' He looked at me and added with a laugh: 'And when you say this, give him your dimmest and most innocent look. You're good at that'. I said nothing.

A remark like that fell into the category of 'Duijvestein humour', a well-intentioned term invented by my father and vigorously taken up by my brothers. I found many of their comments needlessly negative and not funny. This time, too, I did not laugh.

I did notice that my father had not used the word 'stolen', perhaps in order to avoid that I might accidentally repeat it in front of the miller. So, once again, I headed to Nootdorp.

In front of nearly every farm that I passed stood a sign: 'We already have everything. Do not enter. Private property'. Sometimes the text elaborated: '...blankets, clothing, etc.' The barter system had, it seemed, made its way to the countryside, where things were also getting tougher. I thought the sign 'Hoof-and-mouth disease. Do not enter this farm' a nasty choice of text. For my part I did not believe it.

The miller recognized me. After he had poured the wheat through a large funnel, I asked him: 'My father wondered whether the wheat loses weight when it is ground.' 'Of course not', he responded curtly. Perhaps I imagined it, but this visit seemed less friendly than my first.

Figure 32: The windmill in Nootdorp still exists today.

At home the bag was put back on the scale. 'Jan, it weighs *more* than when you left!' called my father out triumphantly. 'I'm glad we spotted that, Jan', he continued. 'He knows that we are friendly with the owner of the mill and so does not want to take any risk. Perhaps it is best that we not tell Meneer Kortekaas anything about this'. I thought it very special that my father used the term 'we'. The word made me feel good.

Another four weeks and it was time to set out again. I walked again to Nootdorp. 'Not enough wind, lad', said the miller when I arrived. For a moment I thought, 'Surely he is not letting me come all this way for nothing, just because we did not trust him?' But there truly was no wind. It was something we should have thought about ourselves.

Of course it was rotten to have to return the next day. That day a hard wind whipped the nasty wet snow fiercely around, making things icy cold. Once again, pancakes had been promised and I focused on that prospect, getting increasingly hungry as I walked.

Because of the icy wind and cold, I decided to take the shorter route, passing without any difficulty the German soldier who, from the vantage point of his little cabin at the highest part of the viaduct, could see very little through the fogged-up windows of his guard box. He probably thought a young boy with a sled, on top of which something was covered with a blanket, not significant enough to warrant leaving the warmth of his box.

When I reached home, I could see my father at the window. He had apparently been watching for me. The door was opened for me, and in the font hall a number of old newspapers were spread out on the floor. 'Jan, would you please stand on top of these papers and not remove your coat yet?' asked my father. Only after a quarter of an hour was I allowed to remove my coat. My father had feared that the sleeves of my coat, stiffly frozen from the cold and icy snow, would rip or break away if I were to suddenly take it off.

Those *pannekoeken* sure tasted good!

Chapter 18
Dutch cigars and boxes of matches

By the start of February 1945, everyone believed in a speedy end to the war. The Germans were losing ground. Even the German-controlled radio announced almost daily proof of losses. 'According to plan, German troops have moved out of the following cities....' The premise, 'according to plan', we did not buy.

All foods were now rationed, available only with tickets. Other items, too, were much harder to come by. At least the allied troops were getting closer and news of their progress fed hope.

While the overall mood was hopeful, there was also bad news. For example, my mother told of a boy picked up during a razzia. He had homemade pins of American, Canadian, and English flags in his pockets. With such pins you could mark on a map the locations of the allied and German troops.

According to her story, the boy had also intended to make German flag pins on the evening before he was caught. But his mother had allegedly said, 'Gosh, it's already so late. Best leave that for tomorrow'. 'If the boy had made the German flags, these too would have been in his pockets when he was picked up. Perhaps his punishment would then have been less severe', philosophised my mother.

Similar stories circulated, including one about a man who received an order to report to the authorities. He had to come in to explain why he had not responded to prior call-ups. When he arrived at the German headquarters, he pretended to be deaf. The German who was interviewing him eventually wrote on a piece of paper: 'You may go'. When the man turned around to leave the office, the German tossed a coin onto the marble floor, which landed with a sharp tinkling sound behind him. The man looked around in surprise and was immediately taken into custody.

During these anxious times, the churches were full, testifying to the Dutch expression: 'crisis teaches prayer'. At home, we were not allowed to complain. There was still enough to eat, even if certain items had become scarce.

One day, my mother informed my father that she needed milk. My father called me to him in his study: 'Jan, I have been thinking', he started, proudly showing me a few large boxes still filled with cigars. 'I managed to obtain these cigars from Meneer De Jong. What if today, you set out...'

And then he described his plan to try to trade a single cigar for a litre of milk on the farms near Leidschendam. He explained how I might best go about this trade. 'Look, Jan, when the farmer says that he's not interested in trading anything and has all he needs, you say "But I have cigars." Then, after waiting a moment, you add "Dutch cigars". Then you wait and see what happens next'. With that last comment he made a face, as if to imply 'That's how you get things done'.

An hour later, armed with just two cigars in a small box, I set out in the direction of the cemetery along the Rodelaan, behind which lay a few farms. I was fully conscious of the immense value of those two cigars; I carried gold!

There was a story circulating that a man walking along the street found himself wondering why there was someone keeping step just behind him. When he turned around to ask why he was being followed, he was told, 'Sir, I walk behind you because I take pleasure in the smoke from your cigar'.

Cigarettes, too, were a much-coveted and costly commodity. I knew that there were cigarettes sold under the term *bukshag*. The word reflected how a person had to bend down, or *buk*, in order to pick up discarded buts from the street, so that they might roll new cigarettes from the leftover tobacco.

Having reached the first farm, I was in such a hopeful mood that I deliberately ignored a large sign that announced 'We already have everything', and rung the bell. The noise of the bell echoed through the farm, which had stone floors. Annoyed by their sign, I thought to myself, 'Well, it sounds like they don't have rugs'.

The front door opened and I saw a roomy vestibule where stood an elderly woman, who with little care for originality repeated, 'We already have

78

everything'. Although I realised that the cigars were unlikely to prove interesting to her, I wanted to exhibit my salesmanship, especially since I'd rehearsed my text throughout the last half hour of walking.

So, I began: 'Yes, but I have cigars—Dutch cigars'. I did omit the pregnant pause, the one that my father had so expertly demonstrated, out of fear that the door was about to close in front of me. Suddenly, from behind the woman opened another door, one with little stained glass squares in it. From behind that inner door appeared the farmer, who had secretly been listening in on our exchange.

Dressed in blue overalls and *klompen*, the man eagerly asked 'Cigars? Dutch cigars?' 'Yes,' I hastily added, 'from <u>before</u> the war'. That last part had not been suggested by my father but seemed to me, having grown up with five years of wartime scarcity, an important aspect to stress.

The farmer took one of the cigars from the box and held it under his nose for inspection, turning and sniffing. He looked to me as if he were playing the harmonica. 'And what do you want for them in exchange?' he asked. 'Milk please, sir', I said.

After I assured him that he was the first farmer that I had approached, he said: 'All right, boy, two bottles of milk for two cigars. And,' he added in a friendly tone, 'if you like, you may return every Saturday'. I promised him that I would.

During the walk back, I suddenly understood why he had wanted to hear that he was the first address I had tried. Even the farmers kept an eye on each other, and apparently it was best to keep silent about the trading of milk for cigars.

Once back along the Laan van Nieuw Oosteinde, an older man, who had been walking a long way behind me, finally caught up with me, slowed as I was by carrying my milk. On his rickety cart lay some winter carrots and a few tomatoes. This was the harvest, apparently, of his own efforts that day.

After walking side by side for a time, he suddenly asked me in a friendly way: 'So, do you have anything to trade'. Even though he probably asked the question with the best of intentions, I was not keen on a long conversation. My 'cigar story' was not one that I wanted to tell to him. After all, I had already succeeded. 'I have matches', I said.

During the first years of the war, my mother had been talked into buying five enormous packets of matches by grocer Veldhoven, who then still delivered door to door. In every packet there were forty or so large boxes that, in turn, each contained twenty-four smaller boxes of matches. Altogether, this amounted to a superfluity of matches that our family could not have used up in twenty years.

'I'll give you two-and-a-half guilders for one box', said the man. Why in the world I had allowed myself to tell this stranger that I had matches with me is something I then asked myself. He had nothing of interest to trade and to take two-and-a-half guilders for one box of matches seemed insane. The original purchase price has likely been a half a cent per box, so that would mean that the man was willing to pay 500 times the cost.

I suddenly found the man a bit pathetic, and the thought flashed through me that I should just give him a box. But that was not possible either, because of what would happen if I came home with the story that I had simply given away a box of matches because I found a man so sad.

At the dinner table I was then sure to be the target of some pointed remarks, such as 'Oh really, well I know of a few more sad souls. What are you going to give them?' I was relieved to find that we had now reached my home and with a 'Goodbye, Meneer' I opened the little garden gate and let myself in.

Chapter 19
Sleepovers in the west country

It was now mid-February in 1945. Not only was there less and less available to eat, even fuel was now scarce. On the Laan van Nieuw Oosteinde, there was hardly a tree remaining. The one just in front of our house was a measure of pride to us, and we took turns 'guarding' it as much as we could. It was a young tree with a diameter of about 15–20 cm.

One evening we saw a few people hunched in the dark around 'our' tree. When one of us opened the front door and shouted 'Hey there, what's going on?' the group dispersed like frightened rabbits.

The tree became a regular topic of discussion during dinner. On one such evening, my father suddenly said, 'Jan, go take a look and see if the tree is still there'. 'The tree is gone', was the sum of my disappointed report when I returned. 'I guess that was inevitable', pronounced my father.

I wondered why we had put so much energy into this topic. Even if the tree had been spared the saw on that particular evening, it would still have come down on the next. I understood why all of the city's municipal trees had to suffer this fate. People were removing pickets from garden gates in front of private homes to burn as fuel for a little warmth. I'd even heard of people stoking fires with the interior doors from their own homes.

A few days earlier, in the Vondelstraat, I'd seen with my own eyes how dozens of people removed the small bricks made from compressed coal dust that lined the space between the rails of the city trams. Those tiny bricks would be useful to anyone with a coal stove at home, almost like a small gift from God.

There were also noticeably fewer dogs about. Naturally, no one at this time would have agreed to acquire a new dog. Families would not welcome an extra mouth to feed. At the start of the war, a story had circulated that Germans rounded up domestic dogs to use in the combing out of minefields. Now, after nearly five years of war, it was rumoured that desperate people were starting to eat even dog flesh.

Figure 33: In many cities bricks made out of compressed coal grit were pried out from between the tram rails and used for fuel. The same was true of the small wooden slats meant to dampen tram vibrations. The robbing out of tram rails was widespread. This picture was taken in the Raadhuisstraat in Amsterdam during the Hunger Winter at the start of 1945. Collection Unifoto via Beeldbank WO2 – NIOD.

One time, I was allowed a sleepover with my uncle and aunt, Oom Jan and Tante Kee, in the agrarian westland. They had a nursery business. I loved pottering about the greenhouses of tomato plants and grapes. It was also a major treat to be allowed, around one o'clock, to join the adults gathered inside the greenhouse to listen to *Radio Oranje* on the BBC station. On one occasion, I even heard the queen, who addressed us as '*Landgenoten....*' After listening to the news from London, the radio would be quickly reburied in the ground and hidden beneath a layer of topsoil.

Figure 34: Queen Wilhelmina addressing her people via Radio Orange from England.

Only after the war did I learn that the electricity for that radio had been sourced from an illegal tap into a German line, buried nearby for the occupiers' exclusive use. If I'd known this when we snuck into the greenhouse for a secret listen then that fact would have further heightened my sense of excitement.

I was disappointed that there was no interest in listening to the messages that followed the official news program. I found them fascinating: '*Tante Sjaan* will arrive one day later' or 'The flowers arrived ok'. Even if I did not understand what was encoded in these phrases, I found it all very exciting.

At night, I slept in their attic. During a previous sleepover, I'd seen the shining parts of at least ten brand new bikes hanging in the rafters. I had not heard any stories about their possession of such bikes and decided it was better not to ask about them.

Years later, my cousin, Wim van der Ende, explained that eventually they'd decided to hide all those bikes, after these became increasingly dangerous to possess. Just before the war broke out, Wim had been asked by our *Oom* Kees, another of my father's brothers, to pick up a shipment of bikes for him as a simple favor. A fellow bicycle-shop owner had asked *Oom* Kees to step in when he could not make a scheduled payment to a dealer for an order of new bikes. *Oom* Kees, who traded in cycles, had agreed to take over the shipment and shoulder the accompanying financial responsibilities. He had asked Wim to pick up the bikes from the train station and, for the time being, store them at the family nursery. In this farming part of the country, a truck loaded with city bicycles would have been an unusual and memorable sight. You never knew if a neighbour from the 'wrong' side might mention something like that to the occupiers.

One evening, when we were all enjoying a shared supper of soup, my cousin Wim asked his mother: 'Mother, we're not having *kroketten* tonight, right? Jan does not like them.' 'You don't like *kroketten*, Jan?' asked my *Oom* with feigned incredulity. I was pretty certain that Wim had told his father about a certain recent event. But I sensed that they all wanted to hear the story directly from my lips, so I began.

Some days earlier, Wim had offered me a *kroket* after explaining that he'd bought them from a friendly butcher. When I asked him if he wasn't afraid that it might contain dog meat, he assured me: 'Oh no, because that's so easy to spot.' 'How?' I'd asked. Wim said that you should hold the *kroket* in front of your face and bark at it like a dog. 'If the *kroket* does not bark back, then it's ok', he'd explained.

I had laughed, but when I bit into my *kroket* I felt quite a few hairs in my mouth and promptly started coughing. 'Wim, what are these?' I asked, showing him the spat-out bite of my *kroket* in which at least five little hairs were distinctly visible. 'Oh, that's just a bit of skin from the cow, which the butcher ground into the meat. That's not gonna kill you.'

I believed him, yet my appetite for that *kroket* was now irrevocably gone. Wim ate them both.

Chapter 20
Far from smart

At night I slept little. The dull roar of airplanes overhead was continuous, and the air was never without that sound. In the mornings, you would find little bits of silver-colored streamers on the street. These were dropped by allied airplanes as a way of drawing enemy fire. In the lights of German antiaircraft guns, these pieces looked like enemy planes. While the Germans wasted ammunition on these little bits of silver, the allied pilots flew in greater safety.

A story made the rounds that the allied pilots had been commanded to drop their load of bombs in Germany, without having been given precise targeting instructions. This meant pilots could release their bombs from a much greater height. That lessened their chances of being shot down by the Germans and increased the odds of a safe return to England. Cities such as Bremen and Berlin were, according to rumour, already completely flattened by bombs.

Since the autumn of 1944, the southern part of Holland had remained largely free—in the wake of the June landings at Normandy. Naturally, everyone followed the fighting closely, although the information we received about this came primarily from the Germans.

Because most people no longer had access to either radio or newspapers, announcements were made available at the newspaper offices. Large chalkboards hung in the windows upon which the news, written in chalk, could be read while standing in the street. Daily, you would see little clusters of people silently reading the information that had been provided to the newspaper offices directly by the German authorities.

One day my father, too, stood among such reading public in front of a newspaper office along the Laan van Meerdervoort, when a young boy suddenly broke the silence. Irked by what he considered the broadcasting of false information, he burst out: 'The Americans are much farther than they admit!' 'You could only know that', said my father, 'if you've been listening to the BBC', and followed it with the German phrase 'Kommen Sie mal mit!' At this point he also grabbed the young man by the collar.

Whether my father's words or his actions caused the greatest dismay is hard to say, but a shockwave went through that little group of bystanders. One heard almost daily of people who were picked up off the street, and now it looked as if this little group was witness to just such an event. The young man in question was white as a corpse and stood as if glued to the spot. 'Boy', resumed my father in Dutch, 'I was merely joking, but you should not talk so much. Talking leads to trouble'. With that he released the young man's collar and wanted to give him a reassuring pat on the back. But the boy was long gone. A sigh of relief went through the little group, along with a lone nod of approval.

It was over morning coffee that my father told this tale. He was visibly pleased with the impact he'd made on the whole assembly when collaring that young man. Strange, but I had formed a very different impression of what had taken place on de Laan van Meerdervoort.

My father had taken such unnecessary risk in playing the role of either a German or a German sympathiser. Surely he was aware of street justice for German soldiers and even sympathisers in broad daylight. Only a month earlier, a German soldier had been *geliquideerd*, or eliminated, on the Laan van Nieuw Oost-Indië and, in turn, the Germans had then shot dead twelve Dutch citizens on that same spot as reprisal.

Why then, as if it was all a great joke, take it upon yourself to play the schoolmaster?

I understood his intention to some extent, but I did not think this a story worth sharing with my friends. My own father, whom I so much admired for that combination of wisdom and street smarts, which he achieved despite a limited formal education, had committed a reckless act.

Only a few days earlier, he'd told me a story and followed it up with a question. My thoughts now returned to that story. 'Jan, last week a German soldier gave himself up to the underground', he'd begun. The German confessed doing wrong and explained how his conscience now demanded that he stop contributing to the war. The soldier had been received with open arms by those in the resistance who had helped him to a safe hiding place.

The Nazi leadership soon contacted *De Ondergrondse*. They threatened to execute half a dozen Dutch citizens whom they had previously arrested and jailed for various and sundry infractions. They demanded that their own deserter be returned to them within 24 hours. If not, they would make good on their threat. So *De Ondergrondse* did turn in the German soldier. 'Surely you comprehend what became of that man?' my father had added.

My lack of sleep was caused not merely by the sound of those airplanes overhead but by stories, like these, buzzing around and around in my mind.

Chapter 21
Sugar beets and tulip bulbs

The eating of sugar beets had become commonplace. Before the war this produce was used almost exclusively in the production of sugar and occasionally fed to pigs. Such had not been the case for a long while.

My family also used sugar beets, and not just to make *stroop*. Sugar beets were now also an important ingredient in the making of *pannekoeken*.

A story made the rounds that throughout the land tulip bulbs were now being consumed as a food. This line was not to be crossed in our house. One afternoon, however, I announced: 'Actually, I'd really like to try them. That way,' I explained, 'I can say after the war that I ate them too'.

The next day, my brothers and I gathered for a tulip-bulb tasting. After first peeling off the papery skin, we cut them into thin slices and lay them on the stovepipe to roast. I don't recall the taste very well. While they did not taste very good, neither were they very horrid.

We'd not seen candy for ages. But I do recall how we often spoke about it. My father, who had a genuine sweet tooth, reassured us regularly that once the war was over he'd spend a whole day eating only bars of chocolate.

Everyone was certain that the war was coming to an end. Yet the occasional story caused flickerings of doubt.

The story about Japanese mini-submarines, steered by a crew who aimed directly at its target and met their own death in the process, I found simply bizarre. Yet many an American warship apparently went down this way. The Japanese believed that if you lost your life in the fighting you would immediately ascend to heaven. This is why, on the day before a son's departure into battle, the families of young soldiers gave a farewell party to celebrate his 'heroic deed'. A pilot would deliberately aim his plane at an American ship in order to make it explode upon impact.

Figure 35: Besides sugar beets, tulip bulbs were increasingly used to supplement rationed food. This photo was taken in Utrecht during the winter 1944–45. Beeldbank WO2 – NIOD – F.W. Bonnet (163575).

Such stories gave way to a nagging feeling that the war might just last much longer than we all had thought.

Chapter 22
Food trips and packets

I had to wake up early one morning. 'Jan, time to get up!' called my mother in a voice that was firm without being stern. 'It's six-thirty', she added as she left the room.

'Well, a half-an-hour gives me plenty of time', I thought. Quickly, I put on my pants and washed my face and hands at the washstand. No bath today because we only did that once a week. I can still hear my father, after all these years, caution us: 'Be sure not to use too much water, because this is plenty', at which point he would spread out his thumb and index finger to indicate the bathwater's desirable height.

My mother had already made me a sandwich and convivially seated herself at the table next to me while I ate. 'For your sake, I hope there won't be too many people today', she said, thinking out loud about my task ahead.

It was not unusual at that time for Meneer Koen, a man of about eighty and a friend of my parents, to ask if Jan (and he always asked for me) could get him a ticket. Every five weeks an auction-boat would take a limited number of passengers from Rijswijk to North Holland, where it would dock somewhere along the coast. That meant passengers had about five hours or so to walk to area farms to try and acquire food. Then the boat would return to Rijswijk.

These boat trips were not, however, without an element of risk. English soldiers were known to aim at any moving vehicle. Our neighbour, Meneer Lasance, had died when his train had been shot at.

Meneer Koen had told us that the sounds of any airplane would prompt the closing of the boat's heavy shutters against an attack, thus leaving those inside in utter darkness. So, I knew this was no pleasure cruise, especially as chances of locating any food had increasingly diminished.

My mother, well able to imagine the difficulties such a trip posed for an old man, had therefore offered to send her son Jan on the previous day to pick up the ticket that would entitle him to a spot on the boat. This at least saved Meneer Koen, already in weakened condition, the trouble of standing in line for a ticket, which could take hours.

Figure 36: Food trips from the city to the countryside were common sights during the Hunger Winter. Beeldbank WO2 – NIOD (198544).

At seven o'clock in the morning, just as people were allowed to go out on the street again, I left our house on foot. Half an hour later, I joined the back of the queue. Luckily, the line did not seem all that long this time. There were a few elderly men, just like Meneer Koen, and also some women.

It was soon made clear to me why the queue was so short. The shipping company had announced that these boat trips would soon cease altogether, and there was even some uncertainty about whether tomorrow's boat would make the journey. The overwhelming reason for ceasing the trips was the increasingly disappointing yield. On the last journey, not a single passenger had succeeded in returning to the boat with food.

As if this was about my own money, I asked the bearded man standing beside me how it worked when the boat for which you'd purchased a ticket never departed. He looked at me as if he either did not understand my question or did not want to explore that possibility. In any case, he did not answer.

Behind me, a woman turned to her neighbour in line: 'Are you feeling ok?'

'No, not really', he responded. At least deafness was not the problem.

'Come and have a rest on this little wall here', said the woman while she supported him by the arm and walked him to a nearby low brick structure. The man could hardly lift his own feet and shuffled slowly along with her help. I'd begun to be rather used to skinny people, weakened or otherwise in bad health.

Suddenly there was a little movement in the line of people and twenty minutes or so later I had my ticket. As I passed the row of people still waiting, I spotted among the last ten persons the woman who had so stoutly helped my neighbour in line. He was nowhere to be seen.

The woman was speaking in urgent tones and from her body language I could tell that she was relating something important. Almost as if she'd been expecting me, she looked in my direction as if to confirm 'we know each other'. Because of that flash of recognition I dared ask: 'Where did that *meneer* go?' "Oh, the *meneer*... yes, he decided to go home, boy. He was not feeling well, but you'd already seen that, right'.

93

She assumed that I believed her, but I didn't. During the war, I'd learned that you were allowed to tell a lie if it was for a good cause. No adult willingly told a young boy of thirteen that the man whom he'd spoken to only a quarter of an hour earlier now lay dead. Without further comment I headed to the Laan van Nieuw Oosteinde.

'Great that you're back so early', said my father upon my reaching home. 'We've gotten word that another large box from Friesland has arrived'. He added, 'Would you go and pick it up today with Kees?' If posed to a stranger the question might have seemed odd, but to me and my brother Kees his request needed no further clarification. The sender would be Meneer Tromp, from Sneek, a friendly acquaintance of my parents. He was a wholesaler in foodstuffs.

Undoubtedly things were getting tougher in his region too, but compared to the West of the country that area seemed like Valhalla. In the heavily populated west, with its three large cities, it was truly a 'Hunger Winter'. Food coupons provided by the occupiers assigned every person the right to 500 calories per day. You'd think this was just enough calories to prevent starvation, but many people died from hunger.

Meneer Tromp knew of our circumstances and had already sent us five enormous boxes of food, of which we had received two. He was in the habit of sending us a letter prior to shipping such a box via riverboat. In the letter he asked after our health and informed us that we could soon expect another packet to arrive at a local quay's freight office.

After a 'surprise packet' had arrived, my father would sit down to write an elaborate thank-you letter that very evening. 'You should have seen the kids cheer and jump for joy when we opened the box. What generosity. We've none of us seen such tasty delights in years', he would write. Even when the promised packet never arrived, my father would write a thank-you for the gift that had not reached us.

Chapter 23
The accidental bombing of
Het Bezuidenhout

My father had something of a sixth sense. This was again the case when, on the 3rd of March 1945, he called out: 'Boys, come and look'. He explained while leading us to the front door, 'I've borrowed a handcart for you'. I recognized the large wooden pushcart that I'd used twice before when I'd similarly been sent to collect a large box of foodstuffs shipped by Meneer Tromp.

'Boys, I don't want you to go via the Schenkkade embankment because things are far too restless there'. My brother Kees and I looked at each other and meekly answered, 'Yes, Pa.' We knew what he meant by 'restless'.

Het Haagse Bos was about half a kilometer from our house. In these woods the Germans had, since last September, hidden a launching pad for unmanned missiles, the so-called V-2 rockets. The Germans regularly fired a V-2 at England. The rocket would first shoot straight up in the air for about 500 meters, then make a thunderous horizontal turn, only to disappear over the dunes in the direction of England.

It later proved that from this location the Germans launched over 1,000 such rockets in only seven months. Via their propaganda machine, we were regularly informed about how yet another such rocket had reached its intended target in London.

Almost daily, English bomber planes flew over Het Haagse Bos to try and blow up this launch pad. But the pad was mobile, and with at least six different locations in the woods where it might be placed it was both understandable and disappointing that the English did not manage to silence its roar.

While we understood why our father did not want us to walk via the Bezuidenhout neighbourhood, which edged Het Haagse Bos, we thought his precaution excessive. After all, it would take us only a quarter of an hour to slip through the danger zone and thereby greatly shorten our trip.

On the other hand, we were in no great hurry since the schools had been closed months earlier for lack of coals to heat them in the winter cold. We therefore walked, without grumbling, out of the Laan van Nieuw Oosteinde in order to turn along the Prinses Mariannelaan to reach the Rijswijkseweg. After half an hour, we pushed that heavy cart, side-by-side, up the Geestbrug, swiftly crossing the bridge as if this were our daily task. Luckily the heavy cart, with its two large wheels and old-fashioned wooden spokes, had inflatable tires.

The steady hum of airplanes that had accompanied us for the last fifteen minutes suddenly broke into the sound of heavy artillery fire. Although we were accustomed to quite a bit of that, we still decided to take shelter in the roomy entryway of a chemist shop.

'That is surely the Bezuidenhout area', said one agitated man just leaving the shop. The sounds grew louder and we knew, even without being told, that what we were hearing were bombs being dropped. 'That's Het Bezuidenhout', the man repeated, adding: 'Every day is target practice there'. 'But we live close by there and have never heard anything like this', one of us offered.

After a further ten minutes of sheltering in that entryway, Kees and I decided to turn around and go home. The stranger said something along the lines of 'You can just as easily keep on going. This will stop any moment!' Without paying any further attention to the man, we turned the pushcart around and headed back over the bridge.

After about half a kilometer we traveled under the viaduct that led to the start of the Laan van Nieuw Oosteinde. There were suddenly a lot of people. It was as if a giant soccer game had just let out!

Kees and I were the only ones heading in the direction of the Bezuidenhout area, and this slowed our progress. It was hard to push the handcart against the flow of this human stream.

Suddenly I spotted my classmate Henk van der Zanden, walking alongside his mother. He saw us too and told me in less than two agitated minutes what had happened. 'Bombs fell out of the sky like ripe apples', said Henk, who thought it pure idiocy to head in that direction. 'You really should stay away from there', added his mother while she pulled Henk along by his coat.

That's when I remembered how the Van der Zanden family had extra reason to be frightened, since they had witnessed the bombing of Rotterdam on 14 May 1940. That's when his family had moved to Den Haag. Henk had been the only boy in our class to give a speech titled 'A real bombardment'.

In our school's hallway hung a large colored print depicting a biblical story, with underneath it the caption 'The Exodus from Egypt'. I thought of that poster when the crowds thickened and it became harder and harder for Kees and myself to move against the current of people.

My father was already at our little gate, watching for us. Only half an hour earlier, while sheltering along the Prinses Mariannelaan, we'd briefly imagined things being not so very bad; we now knew better.

'So glad you're back', my father greeted us. Without any further question or comment, he ran back into the house. Within minutes a number of suitcases and bags were placed on the cart and our whole family, visibly nervous, set off—after my father managed to drop off the front door key with the neighbours.

Our younger brothers took over the pushing of the cart, and the whole crew headed in the direction of the old town of Voorburg. I walked next to my mother, who brought me up to date on what was happening. We were to stay for a few days with the Verhoef family. They lived in a large house called 'Merelwijk' that lay along Oosteinde at number 199.

I wondered how my father had arranged all this so quickly. He must have consulted them ahead of time somehow. Surely you could not show up with nine people on someone's doorstep without checking with them first.

'Must be a nice family', I thought while we marched. I already knew that they were 'good people'. The then-famous singer, Jo Vincent, regularly gave small performances at Merelwijk, with the proceeds going to De Ondergrondse.

Just as we reached the start of the Laan van Nieuw Oosteinde, the sound of a diving airplane scattered the crowd. The front door of the house at number nine stood wide open and people practically fell over each other in their eagerness to get inside. 'Boys, the suitcases!' shouted my father anxiously. 'How can you think of suitcases at a time like this', said a stranger next to him. 'Especially at a time like this!' said my father emphatically, who saw that I'd managed to get inside with one of those suitcases.

But nothing more happened just then and we continued on our journey, arriving at the big house of Merelwijk. It had an enormous attic, which the nine of us put to good use.

After dark that evening, and despite it being *spertijd*, we returned briefly to our own house to pick up a few more things. The crowd now flowed in two directions. Most people walked with carts, or baby carriages, laden with stuff. There was not one German soldier visible anywhere. As we got closer to our own address, the sky grew lighter. The many houses on fire gave off a red–orange glow.

Not a single bomb had fallen on our side of the tracks that marked the border between Den Haag and Voorburg. On the *Haagse* side, however, the whole neighbourhood was lit up and entire city blocks reduced to rubble.

Figure 37: The ruins of homes in Het Bezuidenhout area after the allied bombing. Nationaal Archief, Den Haag, via Creative Commons.

While my father spoke briefly with our neighbours *Meneer* and *Mevrouw* Peeting, my mother rapidly refilled the suitcases and bags. After only twenty minutes, we were heading back to our temporary abode.

My parents decided to return home after only two days. The absence during those two days of any airplane sounds had given the impression that it was safe to return.

Once home, I was curious about the bombing in the Bezuidenhout neighbourhood. Alone, I walked in the direction of school and quickly reached the Amalia van Solmsstraat, the street where my friend Bennie Pas lived. Their house was gone!

I was surprised to see an older brother of Ben's walking across the piles of rock, picking up bricks and tossing them aside again. When he saw me, he spoke in an emotional and hurried manner of how his family had sheltered under the stairs when the bombing began. The sound of an approaching bomb (it had exploded in their backyard) so panicked his mother, Mevrouw Pas, that she ran out from underneath the stairs and had surely died as a result. The rest of the family had survived.

For two days they'd been searching the rubble for their mother but had not yet found her body. I quickly offered to help. 'Then you'd better put these on', said Ben's brother as he handed me a set of leather gloves. I soon understood that these gloves were no luxury. The bricks remained red-hot. After a few hours, I also understood that without proper tools or machinery it was impossible to conduct a thorough search.

After a few more days, mother Pas was eventually found. Frans Pas told me: 'Jan, there was nothing left of her. She could fit into one cigar box'. Those are words I will never forget!

Later, I learned that the bombing of the Bezuidenhout area may have occurred because the 55 allied bombers received the wrong coordinates, leading to a tragedy that ended in streets of flame and smoke. More than 500 people lost their lives, with another 400 missing. At least 30,000 people were suddenly made homeless.

There was also a rumour that the Germans had shot Dutch people who, finding their fellow citizens dead along the road, had robbed their bodies of belongings. They had even pried rings from dead fingers!

When I heard that, I understood why my father had yelled 'Boys, the suitcases!' If people were capable of robbing the dead, surely the grabbing of an unattended suitcase was but a very small transgression!

Chapter 24
Hopes of freedom meet a grizzly end

How my father always managed to be so well informed, I'll never know. But on 7 March 1945 he was excited by the latest news: 'Jan, last night they tried to assassinate Rauter, although the attempt failed!'

Everyone knew who Rauter was. He was a high-ranking member of the SS and the head of the police in those days. He signed a lot of orders, and whosoever failed to follow them risked being summarily executed.

Figure 38: The heavily damaged car belonging to Rauter, after the attack near Woeste Hoeve. Beeldbank WO2 – NIOD (85934).

Even I understood that the failed attempt on Rauter's life, which occurred at Woeste Hoeve in the Veluwe hills would be severely punished. And indeed after a few days we heard how the Germans had rounded up over one hundred prisoners, most of them young men, from all over the country. They'd hauled them to the location of the failed attack, only to shoot them all dead on that very spot.

The previous summer, at least 600 young men from the town of Putten had been picked up in reprisal for an attack on a German army convoy. These men were transported to a German concentration camp, where most of them died. Now it seemed as if the occupiers wanted to punish the entire Dutch populace for this failed attempt on Rauter's life.

Figure 39: The first signage put up as a memorial at Woeste Hoeve on the Veluwe to mark the murder of 117 people. CODA archief.

Although for many weeks now we'd relished the idea that freedom could not be far off, news of the mass killings on the Veluwe made us all realise that our liberation might take much longer.

On the 1ˢᵗ of April 1948, three years after we were liberated, the trial of Hanns Albin Rauter began in the special War Court in Den Haag. During the war, Rauter had been the most feared leader of the Nazi military police. As a result, there were lengthy and multiple public court hearings before final judgment was reached.

Aged sixteen, I wanted to attend a public session in person. While I stood in line outside the courthouse, I started to worry. 'Would the general rule that attendees be over twenty-one be strictly enforced?' 'Should I have brought some sort of proof of identity with me to gain access to the public gallery?'

Figure 40: Hanns Albin Rauter (1895–1949), convicted Nazi war criminal, was executed on 24 March 1949 for crimes against humanity.

I was relieved to recognize Meneer Koos van Gelder among those waiting to enter. He was a famous soccer player who had even played for the Dutch national team. But right then, the fact that he knew my father was far more important to me than soccer. Only a few weeks earlier, my father had introduced us. In order to reach him, I allowed a few people to go ahead of me in line. He recognized me and a few moments later we passed together through heavy entrance doors flanked by guards. No one asked for identification, and my clever attempt to blend in like father and son proved unnecessary.

From my seat in the public gallery there was a great deal that I did not comprehend. The use of the German language, legal terminology, and the great distance between the public gallery and the judicial bench all contributed to my lack of understanding. I nonetheless found it fascinating to think that I was watching someone who would receive the death penalty—because I was certain that would be the outcome. This assumption became fact about a month later, when the judge pronounced the sentence: 'Death by firing squad'.

This gallery experience had long retreated into the background for me when, in March of 1949, I rode the train from Den Haag to Amsterdam. At that time, I worked as an intern at the realty office of Wolf en Luirink, along the Keizersgracht in the center of town. Already seated, my attention was drawn to a small cluster of people gathered in the train's center aisle and blocking the way.

A soldier amidst this group told an elaborate tale of what he had experienced that morning. He took obvious pleasure in the interest that everyone showed for his story. When a few people moved on, I shifted to a seat nearer to the soldier. He mentioned how Rauter, addressing his own firing squad that morning, had been heard to say: 'I wore a clean shirt, just for you'.

The soldier explained that he had been one of the twelve members of the firing squad involved in that morning's execution. Rauter had asked for permission to be allowed to give the final order to fire. This permission had been granted. As I sat on that train, I became increasingly upset that Rauter's final wish for control had been granted him. It seemed to me that this particular man should not be granted any further power!

When the soldier had finished, he looked around as if in official expectation of questions. I broke the silence to ask: 'Do you not fear that, one day, you might think to yourself "Gee, I killed someone"?' Although we looked to be about the same age, he answered me in a tone that suggested he felt himself to be many years my senior. He said: 'No, not at all. And do you want to know why? Because this problem was anticipated'. He could tell by my expression that I did not comprehend his remark and he eagerly continued.

The execution involved a squadron of twelve soldiers. One of them was armed with a gun loaded with 'losse flodder' instead of a real bullet. A 'losse flodder' was a type of wooden bullet, or blank, that virtually disintegrated when a gun was fired. 'And that could have been my gun', ended the soldier with a stern look in my direction. I had no further questions.

Chapter 25
Food drops

Via the *radiodistributie* we heard, at the end of April 1945, that German leadership had given the English permission to fly over the West of the Netherlands to drop food packets from the air. As a condition of this aid, the English had stipulated that the Germans would not shoot down any low-flying airplanes dropping food in designated areas.

Just as soon as it was announced that the planes had left England, people filled the streets. I was among those who climbed the embankment next to the viaduct along the Laan van Nieuw Oosteinde, right near the Laan van Nieuw Oost-Indië. The planes flew over the Bezuidenhout area in the direction of the airfield Ypenburg. Sometimes an airplane made an up and down motion with just the tips of its wings. I was told that this was intended as a greeting of sorts, in response to the waving public and their displays of enthusiasm below.

Figure 41: Cheers for the first food drops over Den Haag in April 1945. Beeldbank WO2 – Resistance Museum Amsterdam (118011).

I thought it absolutely wonderful to stand with so many people on the top of the dike and to be able to wave, unpunished, to the British pilots who were so very close that you could see them sitting in their cockpits! One of these planes dropped a bag of foodstuffs in the soccer field opposite the church called Liduinakerk. By accident or design? Whatever the reason, this field was not one of the German-designated drop zones.

The fact that the Germans had granted the allies permission to fly so very low, blithely risking the chance that they would simultaneously take pictures of potential targets, told me that the Germans were ready to give up. This proved true only a few days later.

Figure 42: Crowds watch a food drop over the city of Den Haag. Beeldbank WO2 – National War and Resistance Museum (143028).

Chapter 26
Liberation

The persistent rumours that the Germans would surrender finally came true on 5 May 1945. Jubilant people everywhere took to the streets, where we all waited for the arrival of American, Canadian, and English soldiers. They were, we heard, only a few kilometers from Den Haag. We wanted so very much to welcome them that we were happy to stand for hours and hours on the side of the road.

Figures 43: Our liberators arrived on the scene in Den Haag. Beeldbank WO2 – NIOD – Menno Huizinga (BC856–HUI–1539).

Parties for young and old sprang up all across the country. We relished all the festivities, temporarily distracted from the fact that five years of war had brought unimaginable suffering for so many people. Many parents had waited in vain for the return of a son transported to work in Germany. This was also when the first messages from the Red Cross reached families whose relatives had died in concentration camps. For the time being we focused on the cheering that accompanied the arrival of allied soldiers. They were so very nice, generously doling out cigarettes and chewing gum.

For hours on end, I stood by the side of the road, admiring convoys of army trucks, occasionally punctuated by tanks—and all of them bedecked with cheering people. That the drivers, despite limited visibility, still managed to keep to the center of the road made a big impression upon me. For the first time in my life I also saw black soldiers, who smiled broadly as they handed out gifts.

Figures 44: Happiness was shared with young and old. Beeldbank WO2 – NIOD – Menno Huizinga (BC856-HUI-185814).

I was annoyed by one Dutchman wearing an orange band on his upper arm, to which he pointed emphatically while begging a soldier for a cigarette. He expected preferential treatment. An orange armband signaled his membership in *De Ondergrondse*, a symbol with which that soldier was undoubtedly familiar. Perhaps this is silly, but I was disappointed that the man's expectations were complied with and that he received two cigarettes. Although I did not know the man at all, I thought of him as an unpleasant sort of fellow.

At the same time as people cheered their liberators, they jeered those who had cooperated with the Germans. Members of the resistance and domestic fighting forces, or *Binnenlandse Strijdkrachten*, pulled any Hollanders known to have sided with the Germans out of their homes. With arms raised, such captives were marched off by armed guards. With every public arrest a little throng would gather, in which many a Dutch citizen found it impossible to refrain from verbalising various ill-wishes towards their countrymen.

During one such tumult, I recognized the man at the center of the group's attention. The guards pushed into his hands a radio discovered in his house and forced him to carry it high over his head. I knew this man! He lived on the Staringkade and had, that previous summer, asked me to participate in the making of a series of photographs about street games popular with Dutch children, such as *priktollen* and *steltlopen*. These pictures were, I'd been told, for a yet-to-be-published book. When I'd dropped by his house afterwards to collect prints, I'd not noticed the illegal radio.

Figure 45: These photos were taken by the German sympathiser known to have staged scenes with neighbourhood kids who, innocent that his true purpose was propaganda, were pleased to have something to do. Left: Me on stilts, with my brother Adri just behind me. Right: My turn at spinning tops, with Adri looking on from far right.

One of the bystanders told me that the man had been secretly employed by the Germans to create promotional images for war propaganda. The photographs he took of us may have been used to demonstrate how Dutch children happily played street games under Nazi rule. We'd been utterly unaware of his true purpose when invited to pose in our Sunday best. From that day onward, I did not attend any more of these little impromptu gatherings.

Having made that decision, I only ever heard about rather than witnessed how young women thought to have fraternised with German soldiers were publicly humiliated and their heads shorn. Men from the *Binnenlandse Strijdkrachten* would pull such women out of their homes and seat them on a stool in the middle of the street where, without any trial or hearing, they were liberated of their hair as onlookers jeered. It is probably unnecessary to point out that such women dared not leave their house for many months afterwards.

Figure 46: Women suspected of having fraternised with German soldiers were publicly shorn and humiliated. Beeldbank WO2 – NIOD.

Chapter 27
Afterwards

We now skip forward a few years. Five years have passed since the war, which thanks to our parents we survived unscathed. Certain decisions made by my father proved of key importance, as the stories I've already told have shown. He was recognized as a man of more than average intelligence. In this context, I recall an anecdote that he proudly related from before the war. It explains how he had been spared from having to serve in the military.

In the year that he received his draft notice there were more eligible young men than deemed necessary, so a lottery was instituted. While my father stood in line to take part in the lottery, he noticed that the two boys ahead of him both picked a lottery ticket from the top layer of the jar. He overheard each of them being told that they had to serve. Both had drawn numbers above 100. My father rolled up his sleeve and dove deep into the jar, retrieving the number 63, which caused him to be excused from military service.

Because of that lucky draw, he also did not receive the call to reenlist in 1939. This left him able to guide his family through the war. That was our salvation. His legendary No. 63 ticket remains in the family, saved as a sort of holy relic. If you look closely, you can see the faded circular mark where for years it was secured in our hallway by a round pushpin.

Figure 47: My father's lottery number became the stuff of family legend.

After five years of deprivation, fear, and solemnity, there was a need for diversion and celebration. Admittedly, our family had made it through the war in relative comfort, as all these stories have attested, especially compared to the tragedies suffered by so many others. But even for us there was, in the wake of the war, a desire to banish hardship and celebrate without restraint. It was as if everyone wanted to make up for the things they'd missed out on.

Figure 48: Official family photo from 1951. Top row: Truus, Pa, Moe, and Kees. Bottom row: Jan, Gerard, Klasien, Jos, and Adri

My parents' silver wedding anniversary was a case in point. The 20th of January 1951 marked my parents' twenty-fifth, and this occasion had to be celebrated in lavish style. For three consecutive weekends, the *Hotel du Passage* witnessed us gather for three separate feasts with family, friends, and business associates. The owner of the hotel, Meneer Jansen, would only later become a friend of my parents, but was immediately impressed by the joyful and civilized nature of the three parties that gathered in his establishment, even though he must have been used to quite a number of partygoers.

Public life had returned to some semblance of normality. Public transportation had resumed. One saw a fair number of cars on the road, and everywhere you looked things were being built.

112

Figure 49: My parents celebrated their silver wedding anniversary over three consecutive weekends in 1951.

Figure 50: My parents in 1955, on a jubilant trip to Milan, Italy, with their youngest sons, Gerard and Jos.

Meneer Tromp, my father's friend, who had regularly sent us food packets from Friesland, had taken the trouble to come and visit us just after the war. My father confessed that he had sent him several thank-you notes for packages that, in actuality, never reached us. He had done this only to keep the packages coming, hoping that some would slip through. His friend confirmed that he would indeed have stopped sending them altogether if he'd known that these things had not reached us. More than 20,000 people lost their lives in West-Nederland during the Hunger Winter, my father recollected. 'But thanks in part to your packages, we survived'. He added with a chuckle, 'too bad that you occasionally wrote the wrong address on the box'. Even *Meneer* Tromp, familiar with the Duijvestein brand of humour, could laugh at this.

In many locations throughout Holland war monuments were erected to remember the fallen. In Voorburg too, along the Zwartelaan, appeared a memorial with the names of fellow villagers killed in the war. Today that memorial stands alongside the Prins Bernhardlaan. From the names carved on this monument I learned that the brother of *Meneer* van Elewout had been executed. I found it impossible to believe that my *Meneer* van Elewout, the baker from on the corner, was dead too, but there was his name—in giant letters carved into stone.

Later I learned that Hendricus Wilhelmus Antonius van Elewout (that was his full name) had been arrested on 21 June 1944 and had afterwards been transported via *Het Oranjehotel* in Scheveningen to camp Vught, and eventually camp Bergen-Belsen. In the concentration camp Bergen-Belsen, he lost his life from illness on 16 April 1945, one day after turning thirty-nine!

Figure 51: The names of H.W.A. van Elewout and his brother W.P. A. van Elewout carved into the monument along the Prins Bernhardlaan in Voorburg.

Since the liberation, our country has held yearly memorial ceremonies where, as per tradition, our national anthem *Het Wilhelmus* is sung. I still do not understand why, more than 65 years after that awful war, we continue to sing the words 'Ben ik van Duitsen bloed', literally 'I am of German blood'. Although I have been told that 'van Duitsen bloed' derives from the old Dutch 'van Dietsen bloed', meaning 'of the people', I still do not fully understand this.

The following is also true...

Whenever I think back on the war, I also experience something almost resembling regret: 'where is that special fellow feeling now?' There was once an atmosphere of unity: 'we belong together and should help each other'. I remember that there were people who stuck a wooden matchstick in the buttonhole of their lapel, with the sulfur head at top. Without a word, they shouted, 'Keep your head up!' To receive such silent encouragement from a total stranger was, for me, a tremendous boost.

Over the decades since, I have become convinced that the shared humanity that I so cherished during the war seems to be slowly disappearing. Do we really need a new common enemy, more hunger, and renewed hardship in order to recognize the value of what we shared?

Figure 52: This is me, Jan Duijvestein, as I looked during the war and while writing this book. The official passport photo was taken in May of 1944, while the other shows me on a trip to Berlin to visit what remains of the Wall.

Looking back: a letter to my granddaughter

Holland, May 2010

Dear Madison,

Naturally, I think back often to the wartime years that I experienced as a young boy. Even if you grow up to be 100 years old, these early years remain the greatest influence upon the person that you become. The household in which you spend your youth is also an important factor.

I remember vividly how every evening all nine of us would linger for hours around the large dining room table, with our father seated at the head. He often led the wandering discussions. While my mother usually did not participate in the conversations, she took visible pleasure in the convivial atmosphere that they generated.

After dinner my father invariably announced: 'Guys, let's all give your mother a round of applause for her fine cooking, which this evening again proved so superb'. It was clear that she appreciated our praise and applause, but she acknowledged it merely with the question, 'Would you like to stay seated for a little while longer, or shall we clear?' More often than not, we'd stay seated to continue the conversation. Sometimes the person telling a story would draw diagrams upon the white tablecloth to illustrate a tall tale.

My father did not need a diagram to explain how war had claimed Holland. That our country had possessed few defensive weapons, we all knew. We also knew the stories that, just before the war, various German clients had told to my father—about the stockpiling of weaponry by the German army. They had added: 'Surely not all of that is just for defensive purposes'.

There had even been individuals who, with their own money, had bought large advertisements in newspapers to warn of the threat of an impending war. Some of these ads read: 'Quo Vadis?' or, in English, 'Where is this heading?' And our government did nothing.

Years later, about 30 years after being liberated by the allied troops, there loomed again the threat of a war in Europe. I often thought of my own youth and the previous anecdotes when my turn came to sit around the dinner table with my own household. Your mother, *Oom* Arjan, and *Tante* Mylène, were then ten, nine, and eight years old. Could they be about to experience what had happened to your grandmother and me in our youth?

The Russians and the Americans, formerly united in their fight against the Germans, were now mortal enemies. At roughly four hours' distance by car was the so-called Iron Curtain. In 1961 in Berlin, the Russians had violated every prior promise and built a cement wall topped with barbed wire through the city, thus hermetically sealing off West-Berlin. I had been surprised that the world had not reacted more aggressively.

The first East-German man who tried to climb over the wall to flee to the West was shot dead by guards and left hanging upon the wall to bleed out. His cries for help to the West were not answered and he died after a few hours.

I did not comprehend the anti-American sentiment that was welling up among a section of the Dutch population. Some swore that America's involvement in the Liberation had only been to serve its own interests. Some thought it ridiculous that Americans wanted to place rockets on our soil to supposedly prevent the coming of another war. What followed was a large anti-American demonstration. 'Quo Vadis?' was my thought, and your grandmother agreed.

I never did ask my own father 'Why, if the threat of war was so obvious, did we never leave?' but I often thought it. History repeats itself, and so when, in 1978, the opportunity came to emigrate, we left on 20 November and arrived that very same day in Los Angeles. No one came to pick us up from the airport because at that moment we did not yet know anyone who lived in America. Your mother can tell you the rest.

Dearest Madison, I wish you the very best.

Opa
IHVJ

Glossary

Banketbakkerij: a type of bakery that specializes in cakes and confections

Borstplaat: a pale, fudge-like, sugary treat that may be shaped into circles, hearts, or even animals when sold at a *banketbakkerij*

Bos: wooded area

Brug: bridge

Bukshag: cigarettes rolled from the leftover bits of tobacco gleaned from discarded butts. To *buk* is Dutch for the verb 'to bend down', and the name wryly reflects how the tobacco is sourced from buts picked up off floor or street.

Das Englandspiel: German for 'The England Game'. This was a large scale counter intelligence operation led by the Nazis. Allied resistance agents operating in the Netherlands were captured and their codes used to fool the Allies into continuing to provide their agents with information and supplies. About 50 Allied agents were captured, manipulated, and executed in this manner.

Dolle Dinsdag: the so-called Mad Tuesday occurred on 5 September 1944. Rumours of the Allies having freed all of Holland caused premature celebrations. The north would have to wait until 5 May 1945 for their liberation. Some of these rumours were not just ill-informed but deliberately spread by the Dutch resistance in the hope of panicking occupying Germans to flee.

Fahrräder: German for bicycles

Fietsen: Dutch for bicycles

Heer: Lord; also used as honorific in formal Dutch manners of address

Herr: German for Mister; used in the same way that 'Mr.' precedes a surname in English

Jan Hagel: a type of gingerbread cookie topped with sugar flakes and almond shavings

Jood/Joden: Jew/Jews

Kolenkachel: small coal-fed heater

Klompen: wooden shoes worn by farming folk in Holland, where soggy soil makes leather shoes impractical in the fields

Kroketten: Dutch croquettes are made of ground or pulled cooked meat that prepared in a thick ragout (the flour base serves as an adhesive of sorts) and, after cooling, rolled into little cylinders. Covered in seasoned breadcrumbs, these savory cilinders are fried in oil and eaten while still warm.

Kwartetspel: Quartets; a card game similar to Go Fish

Laan: lane or street; common Dutch term for a large city throroughfare

Landgenoten: fellow countrymen

Meneer: Dutch for Mister; used in the same way that 'Mr.' precedes a surname in English

Mevrouw: Dutch polite form of address for an older or married woman. When used by itself, it functions like "ma'am" in English, and when used with the surname it works like 'Mrs.'

Mina Bakgraag: the name of a portly cartoon figure introduced on packages of flour in 1942 by the Dutch firm of Peja. The literal translation of her name is 'Bake-happy Mina'.

Moffen: ethnic slur for people of German descent. The closest English equivalent is Kraut.

N.I.O.D.: acronym for '*het Nederlandse Instituut voor Oorlogsdocumentatie,*' which translates into the Dutch Institute for War Documentation

N.S.B.: acronym for Nationale Socialistische Beweging, a Dutch fascist-turned-socialist political party that existed from 1931–1945. Members of this party were known to sympathise and cooperate with the Nazis.

De Ondergrondse: Dutch resistance movement, or The Underground

Oma: grandma

Oom: uncle

Het Oranjehotel: The Orange Hotel; a colloquialism for the prison in Scheveningen where Germans held and interrogated many Dutch citizens. The color orange is associated with the Dutch royal family and is therefore a national symbol.

Pannekoeken: Dutch pancakes are traditionally eaten for dinner rather than, as in the United States, for breakfast. *Pannekoeken* resemble thick French crepes in that they do not rise when cooked and may be as large as dinner plates. Traditionally, *pannekoeken* can be either sweet (e.g. with apples baked in) or savory (e.g. with bacon), and are eaten with a drizzle of *stroop*.

Priktollen: old Dutch game of 'whip tops' in which a wooden spinning top is kept in motion with a small whip

P.T.T.: acronym for *Post Telegraaf Telefoon*, the nationalized postal and wire-services company

Radiodistributie: name for the distribution of small radio receivers by the Germans to replace confiscated radios. These new radios could only receive the two stations sanctioned and controlled by the occupiers.

Radio Oranje: From London, the Dutch queen addressed her own people via BBC broadcasts in a Dutch-language program called Radio Orange.

Razzias: raids

Rauter: Nazi Chief of Police, SS General Hanns Rauter (1895–1949), who was eventually captured by the British Army and turned over to the Dutch. Tried for war crimes and sentenced to death, he was executed by firing Squad on 24 March 1949.

Samenschoolingsverbod: Dutch word for the German-imposed rule that forbade gatherings of more than three people

Scheveningse scheepsbeschuit: literally, this tongue-twister means 'shipboard-biscuits from the town of Scheveningen'. It was said that this difficult phrase became a litmus test for native speakers, since the challenging pronunciation could trip up any German feigning to be Dutch.

Spertijd: curfew. During the German occupation it became illegal to be out of doors between designated nighttime hours (Jan mentions the hours between 10 pm and 7 am). Curfew times in occupied Holland started with a general rule to stay indoors between midnight and 4 am but soon varied from city to city and could be altered with little notice.

Steltlopen: Dutch term for walking on short wooden stilts, a game for children

Stroop: a sweet, thick, dark syrup traditionally made of sugar (derived from beets) and flavored with fruits such as apples. As a sweetener, it is used in cooking and even drizzled on bread. Think of it as a cross between molasses and honey.

SS: abbreviation for the German *Schutzstaffel*, the paramilitary arm of the Nazi party.

Tante: aunt

Verboden: not allowed, or forbidden

Vught and *Bergen-Belsen*: two separate Nazi concentration camps. Bergen–Belsen, where Meneer van Elewout dies from illness on 16 April 1945, was also where Anne Frank and her sister Margot died of typhus in March 1945.

Wilhelmus: title of the Dutch national anthem. It is the oldest national anthem in the world, with a performance history that dates back to 1568. The anthem is written from a first-person perspective, as if sung by William of Orange himself, and reflects the political loyalties operating during the sixteenth century.

Woeste Hoeve: a location near Apeldoorn, where fighters from the Dutch resistance shot at the Nazi Chief of Police, Hanns Rauter, on 6 March 1945. The shooting occurred during the attempted capture of a German food truck. Huge reprisals followed. 116 Dutch men were rounded up and shot on the spot at Woeste Hoeve itself. A further 147 prisoners held by the Gestapo, or German secret police, were executed elsewhere.

CPSIA information can be obtained
at www.ICGtesting.com
Printed in the USA
BVHW062232240520
580162BV00001B/1